SPYGATE

The Untold Story

Copyright © 2012 Bryan O'Leary. All rights reserved.
No part of this book may be reproduced in any manner whatsoever without written permission except in the case of brief quotations embodied in critical articles and reviews.
For information, contact:
klrpublishing@spygatebook.com
Manufactured in the United States of America
10 9 8 7 6 5 4 3 2 1
Edited by Anna Nething
Book Design by Anthony Sclavi & Ryan Nygard
Book Artwork by Andra Cobb
International Standard Book Number
ISBN 13: 978-0-9854670-0-5

*For my four lovely ladies,
who have got me surrounded.*

Surrounded in love, hope and laughter.

KLR Publishing

Dallas, Texas

The obscure we see eventually.
The completely obvious,
it seems, takes longer.

–Edward R. Murrow

Table of Contents

Introduction — 11

A National Scandal Breaks
Section I — 15

Caught Red-Handed
Chapter 1 — 17

The NFL Cover-up
Chapter 2 — 35

The Players
Section II — 59

Tom Brady
Chapter 3 — 61

Bill Belichick: A Coaching Legend is Born
Chapter 4 — 75

Who is Ernie Adams?
Chapter 5 — 89

Spygate Demystified
Section III — 103

The Matt Walsh Interviews
Chapter 6 — 105

The Patriot Way – Black Ops
Chapter 7   131

Say It Ain't So, Josh!
Chapter 8   161

Why No Love for Brady?
Chapter 9   177

Statistical Anomalies
Section IV   195

Background for Statistical Analysis Chapters   197

Home Game Records
Chapter 10   205

Perfect at Home
Chapter 11   213

Against The Spread
Chapter 12   223

Conclusion   237

Acknowledgements   247

Appendix A
All Endnotes   251

Appendix B
Catalog of Figures and Tables   267

Appendix C
NFL Home Records 2001–2011   269

Appendix D
ATS NFL Wins 2001–2011   275

Introduction

Spygate? What is Spygate? Spygate is the name the media attached to the National Football League cheating scandal that was uncovered during a New England Patriots vs. New York Jets game on September 9, 2007. The media has a funny way of attaching "gate" to all modern scandals, a nod to Watergate.

The NFL fined the New England Patriots a total of $750,000 and stripped the team of a first round draft choice. Both are maximum penalties. The Patriots admitted to the practice of taping opposing coaches for over six full seasons.

Many fans and observers are misinformed about this incident. Was this a case of lip reading, taping of coaches, or bugging of locker rooms? They are misinformed for a variety of reasons. Some people don't really care. Some are too busy with their lives or other important news stories. But most are misinformed because the National Football League wants it that way. And for reasons no one can understand, the media has been missing in this controversy, and the story went largely uninvestigated. The NFL would have fans believe the Patriots developed an elaborate cheating mechanism (herein, *Spygate system*) and that

SPYGATE

it had no effect on the outcome of the games the Patriots won while using it.

This is the first book dedicated to uncovering exactly what the New England Patriots were doing for six seasons, while winning three Super Bowls and setting numerous NFL records.

Even a casual fan will notice that nearly all sportscasters and media members speak of the New England Patriots with reverence, as though the cheating incident never occurred. This leaves fans wondering,

> *What really happened there? Are the Patriots really what they seem to be?*

This book is a counter narrative to the "official story" the NFL's commissioner and team owners have been selling to the public for years. This book will take the reader through the Spygate incident itself, from media reports done at the time. The reader will then clearly see the NFL cover-up in all of its obvious clumsiness. Then the reader will be taken through the backstory of the three most important players in this scandal. Tom Brady, some say, is "the best quarterback to ever play in the NFL." We will follow Tom from his high school days to present. You will read of Bill Belichick's rise to stardom through a perspective you have never been shown. And most importantly, you will learn the existence of a mysterious character, a Svengali who runs the Patriots from the shadows, hidden from nearly every hard-core NFL fan...until now.

You will read testimony from an actual videographer who shot some of the illegal tapes; he will explain how the system worked. The system will be explained in a way that will shock and surprise nearly every fan—you may never watch an NFL game the same way again. This story will connect the dots as no one else has done. Original theories will be supported by mountains of corroborating evidence, including testimony from ex-Patriots players and coaches. You will even hear from an ex-United States Senator, as well as the foremost authority on sports gambling in the United States.

The book concludes with a section on statistical analysis that will supply the reader with ample evidence of the potency of the Spygate system, and the effect it had on the Patriots' success.

This is my first book. I am a fan just like you, a soccer dad from the Southwest. I have written this because others would not. All of the facts are sourced; I invite you to check them all. I hope you enjoy the ride. Good luck to your team this season, and God bless!

A National Scandal Breaks

Section I

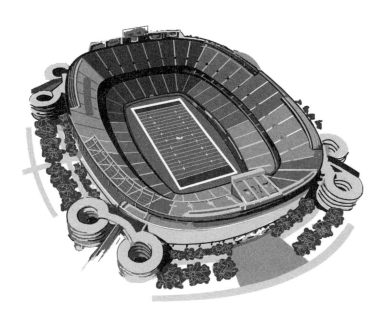

Caught Red-Handed

Chapter 1

The opening day of the 2007 National Football League season was September 9th, and familiar foes were featured in the day's action. The New York Jets would face their archrival, the New England Patriots, at Giants Stadium in East Rutherford, New Jersey. The first Sunday of an NFL football season is a day millions of fans anxiously await; this first day of the season is always exciting. After all, everyone is undefeated, hopes are high, and the future holds unlimited promise.

The Patriots were coming off a successful 2006 campaign in which their record was 12-4. They advanced to the AFC Championship game, losing to the eventual Super Bowl Champion, the Indianapolis Colts. Earlier in those same playoffs, the Patriots had eliminated the Jets during the Wildcard round. In fact, the Patriots, led by Tom Brady, had been having their way with the Jets for some time. As the Patriots' quarterback, Brady was 7-0 against the Jets at Giants Stadium, and 11-2 overall. Brady was so consistent he had thrown for seventeen touchdowns against only five interceptions during that span of games.

Coaching the Jets was relatively young 35-year-old Eric Mangini, in only his second year as head coach of New York's Gang Green. It was a classic matchup of teacher versus pupil. The Patriots' head coach was NFL coaching legend Bill Belichick, who had been the master and idol of Eric Mangini for years. Mangini had such respect for Belichick that he named his second son William. Mangini worked under Belichick for years, starting as a ball boy at age 23 and serving as an assistant coach for nine years.

Without Belichick, Mangini likely wouldn't have had the opportunity to be the Jets' head coach. Mangini spent only one year as defensive coordinator for the Patriots. However, in that brief time, he was given the nickname "Mangenius" for his ability to produce impressive defensive performances from players who were unheralded and, in many instances, had never previously played together. In 2005 the Patriots set an NFL record for the highest number of different starting players for a division-winning team. In football, eleven men play eleven men; due to injuries, those Patriots amazingly started forty-five different players during one season. Regardless of which player the Patriots' defense lost to injury, the next man stepped in and played well.

Mangini had taken the New York Jets to the playoffs in his first season as head coach and the pressure was on to prove that season was not a fluke. On opening day 2007, he faced his old mentor, Bill Belichick. This game was personal for both coaches due to their history together and something was brewing beneath the surface. What the fans didn't know was that behind the scenes, there was a secret both men shared. This secret would ultimately rock the foundation of the NFL and polarize the sports world. It was the type of secret, that once revealed, would change reputations forever.

Eric Mangini knew from his time coaching with Belichick that the teacher was using a system that would give the New England Patriots an unfair advantage against his Jets. Coming off the loss to the Patriots in the playoffs, Mangini simply could not stand for it any longer. Therefore Mangini set a trap, by instructing Jets security to look for Matt Estrella, a Patriots video assistant. Matt Estrella had one job and one job only on game days: to shoot footage of the opposing team's defensive coaches as they signaled in the defensive plays. While the game is in progress, sideline coaches often give signals and hand gestures to the players on the field.

Note that Mangini could have easily instructed Jets security personnel to simply shut down Estrella's filming once they spotted him, as filming opposing coaches' signals is a clear violation of the NFL rules. Instead, Mangini allowed Estrella to illegally tape his coaches for a short time, so there was sufficient video evidence ensuring there would be no question of intent or guilt. Once Jets security had apprehended Estrella, they handed the tape to NFL security and sources ultimately confirmed there was clear, visual evidence of the Patriots' violation. [1]

During the ensuing game, the Patriots were also found to be in violation of exceeding the number of radio frequencies they were allowed to use during a game. When asked directly about this, the Patriots did not have a satisfactory explanation about these possibly illegal communications. [1]

These potentially major violations were ultimately picked up by media outlets and were publicly discussed for several weeks.

SPYGATE

However, considering the seriousness of these violations and the ultimate advantage these types of actions could provide, the NFL's response, the overall media coverage, and the penalties given to the New England Patriots were suspiciously nominal. If not for the excellent and nearly solitary effort of ESPN's Chris Mortensen, these facts may have been buried forever with limited exposure. The question any NFL football fan should ask is whether these activities, over the years, played a major factor in the success of one of the most heralded franchises in NFL history, the New England Patriots.

The information I will share throughout this book should help shed light on those questions, and may simultaneously create many more.

The Patriots won that game against the Jets 38-14, which was also Randy Moss' first game as a New England Patriot. This would be the beginning of an amazing statistical season for the Patriots offense. However, that was inconsequential at this point—a national scandal had broken. When news of the illegal taping incident became public, NFL fans everywhere were shocked.

Why would the Patriots coaches need to tape the Jets' defensive signals? The Patriots always beat the Jets, didn't they? Could this mean that all of the Patriots' recent achievements were due to stolen information and deception? How long had the Patriots been doing this? Was the legend of Belichick and Brady a fraud? After all, the coach and quarterback had just authored one of the most amazing NFL turnaround stories ever written.

After years of disappointment, the Patriots hired Bill Belichick before the 2000 season. Merely one year later, he won the Super Bowl. Even more remarkable was that they were led to the Promised Land by an overlooked sixth round draft pick as their quarterback. It was an amazing reversal of fortune that took the Patriots from last place in their division to holding the Lombardi Trophy in one year.

The Patriots quickly added two more Super Bowl wins, becoming the only team to win three Super Bowls in four years. It was like a fairytale. But now, no one knew what to believe.

The rule the Patriots had violated in the NFL Game Operations Manual states:

> *"No video recording devices of any kind are permitted to be in use in the coaches' booth, <u>on the field</u>, or in the locker room during the game… All video shooting locations must be enclosed on all sides with a roof overhead."* [2]

This implies that any cameras should be in a booth, not down on the field. In this case, a New England Patriots video assistant was caught shooting from the Patriots' <u>sideline</u>, so NFL security officials confiscated the camera and videotape. To be sure, taping a coach's signals is clearly prohibited.

The reaction from Patriots owner Robert Kraft was unsettlingly vague. *"When you're successful in anything, a lot of people like to try to take you down and do different things. We understand that."* Kraft told reporters this at a charity appearance just days later. [1] His team had been caught red-handed and yet he was playing the victim.

Belichick's response was hard to comprehend. Not only did he seem unapologetic (even in his apology), he genuinely seemed annoyed that anyone would question him about this scandal. He issued the following statement before his press conference.

SPYGATE

"Although it remains a league matter, I want to apologize to everyone who has been affected, most of all ownership, staff and players," Belichick stated, *"Following the league's decision, I will have further comment."* [3]

Those further comments never came.

His press conference soon after was bizarre. The video of the press conference is still on YouTube. The following transcript is very close to a verbatim account of the press conference.

Author comments in brackets.

> **Reporter:** Coach, how long have you been taping defensive coaches?
>
> **Belichick:** I misinterpreted the rules. I made a statement, it speaks for itself.
>
> **Reporter:** Aren't you putting the players in an awkward position by not discussing this?
>
> **Belichick:** Said all I can say.
>
> *[You haven't said anything, at all.]*
>
> **Belichick:** Any questions about the Chargers?
>
> *[The next Sunday's opponent]*

Reporter: But the rules say "no recording on the sideline" and you even got a notice clarifying that. How could you misinterpret that?

Belichick: I think we're getting ready for the Chargers. The Chargers are my concern. [4]

[That's it. No comment?]

Belichick's demeanor appears evasive and clearly not apologetic. He seems downright irritated that the reporters won't drop the subject.

It was like he was a New York City traffic cop at the scene of an accident. *Nothing to see here folks, let's move it along…*

But there was more to see, a lot more.

Coach Belichick's position, we would learn, is that he "misinterpreted" a rule. The rule he was specifically referring to states:

> *"Any use by any club at any time, from the start to the finish of any game in which such club is a participant, of any communications or information-gathering equipment, other than Polaroid-type cameras or field telephones, shall be prohibited, including without limitation videotape machines, telephone tapping, or bugging devices, or any other form of electronic devices that might aid a team during the playing of a game."* [5]

He leaned on this in-game language: "during the playing of a game." In his odd interpretation, taping signals was fine as long as you used it in the next game and not in the actual game you were taping.

SPYGATE

Some members of the northeastern press entertained Belichick's determined opinion of the language being ambiguous. When reporters asked Jeff Fisher, then Tennessee Titans head coach and member of the competition committee, whether there was a need for clarification, he was not amused. "The rules are very, very clear, there is no need to be more specific or to clarify any rules whatsoever," Fisher said. [6]

Indeed, only a morally flexible person would argue that it was acceptable to tape and decode a private signal for the express purpose of using it in a contest of wits. After all, the point of using signals is that only your team, coaches, and players know what they mean. Using knowledge of your opponents' signals in any game would allow you and your players to know what your opponent is about to do next; a practice known worldwide as cheating. Everyone knows what cheating is; most people don't need a rules manual. Most casual fans who watch professional football may think that football is a game where fast and powerful men run at each other, trying desperately to knock each other down. That is not what the game football is, at all. Football is a chess match; a game where, like war, one team tries to exploit their opponent's weaknesses. It is through that successful exploitation one will be victorious. Sure, being powerful and fast is important. But the X's and O's give you a strategic edge that is far more important than brute force or blazing speed. If team A is facing an opponent with much more powerful players, team A could still win the game if they are proficient where team B is weak. For example, consider that team A has one great wide receiver, and they play another team with average defensive backs. Team A's receiver could score three touchdowns and win the game, no matter how powerful the other team is in all the other phases of the game. Hence the phrase "football is a game of matchups."

Knowing what your opponent will do next is clearly a huge advantage that will change the basic tenets of the game. No NFL fan would watch a game if espionage was part of the outcome. Surprise and timing are what make football like a battle, a mini war where strength and speed are combined with strategic game planning. It's a game of situational adjustments. Bill Belichick knew this better than most. His father was a celebrated scout and coach for the Naval Academy. Watching his dad, he spent his whole life drawing up X's and O's for the expressed purpose of gaining strategic advantage in situational football. Belichick is not a motivational coach, like Bill Parcells or Jimmy Johnson. He is not a "rah-rah" in-your-face kind of leader. Anyone can see from his interviews that his communication skills are hardly peppy or charismatic; he speaks in a monotone voice with a gloomy temperament. Belichick's whole philosophy of coaching is to strategically put players in a position to win. Simply put, his teams win because of his strategic advantage.

Belichick's statement about the tapes never being used during the game was critical to his defense. Not that it held much sway with anyone else. He could not have known at the time that an ex-Patriots employee would eventually turn over several defensive signal tapes, including one of a 2002 AFC Championship Game featuring the Patriots and the Pittsburgh Steelers. [7]

Naturally, since they would not see Pittsburgh again that year, there would be no need to tape that game if, as Belichick suggested, the tapes were never used during the very game being taped. The underdog Patriots won this game on the way to their first unlikely Super Bowl win. Backup quarterbacks don't usually win the Super

SPYGATE

Bowl in their first year starting in the NFL, as Tom Brady would do.

In that AFC Championship game, almost to prove the point, Brady, who was having a great day, was injured before halftime and his replacement, Drew Bledsoe, also had similar success against the league's number one defense. It was as though it didn't matter who the quarterback was, as long as they were checking down to the right offensive calls. The fact that the players are interchangeable as long as the Patriots' "system" is working is an important point that will be explored further in later chapters.

This Spygate taping incident at the Jets game was not the first time the Patriots had been caught taping the signals of opposing coaches. In 2006, Green Bay officials removed a New England cameraman from the sideline during the Patriots' 35-0 victory at Lambeau Field. As word filtered through league channels that year, Indianapolis officials were suspicious enough to remove all non-network cameras from the RCA Dome before the Colts and Patriots played in the 2006 AFC title game. [2] In addition, the *New York Times* reported that the Patriots had been spotted taping the Giants defensive assistant giving signals in the final preseason game of 2006. [6] This incident prompted a letter from NFL official Ray Anderson warning teams and detailing the interpretation of the rules. Anderson's letter stated:

> *"Videotaping of any kind included but not limited to taping of an opponent's offensive or defensive signals is prohibited on the sidelines, in the coaches' booth, in the locker room, or at any other location accessible to club members during the game."* [8]

In other words, "No taping signals—ever"! Essentially, the memo was addressed specifically at Belichick and the Patriots. Belichick had been directly warned by the league to stop cheating. He was unfazed. The information he was gathering must have been too important to him and the team's success, or he would have stopped, keeping his spying a "league" secret.

As public opinion was turning against him, Belichick agreed to sit down with CBS Investigative Correspondent, Armen Keteyian. The interview is still on YouTube and well worth a look. [8]

Several important details emerge right from the horse's mouth, so to speak. After his standard line claiming the Patriots did not use the tapes "in the same game," Keteyian reminded Belichick of the NFL's special memo explicitly ordering him (and other coaches) to stop all taping of signals. Belichick stated in response, "Again, I go back to the Constitution and Bylaws. That overrode it. I interpreted it incorrectly. I was wrong." Was Belichick stating that after being told by NFL officials in unambiguous terms to stop taping opponents' sideline signals, he instead relied on the ambiguous original Bylaws to cover him, as the Patriots continued to cheat? "I guess I should have called and asked them (the NFL), that was my fault," said Belichick. [8] He said he should have called the league and asked, *Please clarify the recently-released crystal-clear notice that states no taping of signals, at any time.* Perhaps he should have asked them, *But we really need these signals, can we keep taping anyway?* Instead of making that call, apparently Belichick decided to go ahead and tape more signals at his games.

He actually said that with a straight face. Now caught doing the exact thing the NFL warned him not to do, Bill's response: *My bad.*

Note: In watching the video, it appeared that Keteyian was helping Belichick give correct or corrected answers. (The news media had been mysteriously missing in this controversy from the beginning.) And still, Belichick got away with making claims not even a close friend would believe. The CBS "investigative" reporter's last question was shockingly disappointing. Keteyian closed the interview by asking, "Since I'm here, is there anything else you'd like to say about this, to put this to rest, so to speak?" Keteyian was sitting in front of a central figure in a massive conspiracy, who had been stonewalling the press since the story first broke. This supposed "investigative journalist" had Belichick all to himself, but foolishly allowed him to answer questions nonsensically, without challenging him. Then Keteyian wanted to "put this to rest"? This controversy had just started, had far-reaching consequences, and the CBS reporter wanted the accused to have the last words, to put this story to rest—hard to fathom.

It is also critically important to note that Belichick admits that "Research Director" Ernie Adams, a person who will loom large in this controversy, decoded the signals. Belichick states, "Ernie looked at them [the tapes]. At times there was some information that came out of it, he used it. That's how it was done."

A key strategist of the New England Patriots decoded signals of opponents and used the data to help them win games. In spite of Belichick's insistence that this process was not done during the same game, that point is hardly worth mentioning.

"Some information came out of it," Belichick says. Well, the natural result is that every defensive signal of the opposing team would be decoded and used for the rest of that game and any other game against the same opponent that season. A fully taped game is not needed to decode basic defensive formations; one quarter of action would suffice. How could anybody with any sense of fairness conclude this is part of normal game preparation? Also note "he used it" in Belichick's statement, meaning Ernie Adams used the information. How does a research director "use" any information during a game?

Four days after the incident occurred, September 13, 2007, the NFL issued an Emergency Mandate ordering the Patriots to turn over any tapes or signal-stealing material gathered in violation of league policy. On the very same day, the league issued its punishment, before they had even seen the tapes or knew the level at which the cheating occurred.

The NFL league office and commissioner Roger Goodell concluded in a letter to the Patriots:

> *"This episode represents a calculated and deliberate attempt to avoid longstanding rules designed to encourage fair play and promote honest competition on the playing field."* [9]

In other words, the NFL concluded that Belichick knowingly cheated after looking at one tape of just one game, the Jets game. His actions were dubbed "a deliberate attempt to avoid longstanding rules...and promote honest competition." Belichick and the Patriots organization had not been competing honestly. The NFL would soon learn the Patriots had been competing this way for seven years. [10]

The NFL fined Belichick the league maximum of $500,000 to be paid personally, not by the team. The team was fined an additional $250,000; since Bill Belichick had so much control over football operations, he was a de facto agent of the team, making the Patriots separately liable. Candidly, a fine of $250,000 to an NFL team is about as punitive as taking one Coors Light from a fan.

SPYGATE

The commissioner also ordered the team to give up next year's first round draft choice if they reached the playoffs, and a second and third pick if they did not. It seemed odd that the draft choice penalty would become a later round if the Patriots missed the playoffs, potentially softening the fine a year later when most people would not notice. Most observers thought this discipline was far too light—a light slap on the wrist—considering that the Patriots might have stolen three Super Bowl trophies with this technology.

The NFL also dutifully stated that Goodell believed Patriots owner Robert Kraft was unaware of Belichick's actions. [3] How could Goodell possibly know that? Did Kraft ask him to say that, perhaps? After all, Goodell works for the owners, not the other way around.

It seemed unjust to many observers that the coach was not suspended for at least one game. Losing a first round pick, while valuable, was not a huge loss, as the Patriots possessed two first round picks in the 2008 draft. They had received a first round pick in a trade with the San Francisco 49ers. So the Patriots still retained a first round pick in the 2008 draft even after the penalty. Ultimately, the penalty amounted to a few dollars from some very rich men. That was it. Case closed.

The biggest mystery of all, one that will no doubt haunt Belichick for the rest of his days, is why he would cheat in a game against one of his closest friends, an ex-Patriots coach, who had intimate knowledge that the Patriots used an illegally obtained tape in every game. Both men knew of the illegal taping system the Patriots had perfected. Belichick should have suspected that Mangini would be aware of this, and would not appreciate being taken advantage of in this way. His actions are baffling; why not try to win just this one game without cheating? This fact speaks volumes about how important the stolen signals had become to the Patriots coaching staff and Belichick personally.

An ex-Patriots videographer, Matt Walsh said "They [The Jets] tried to catch [Belichick] the year before [2006] but couldn't." [11] The Patriots were so full of hubris the following year that they tried to cheat right under the noses of former Patriots coach Mangini and NFL officials who had already issued a warning.

Patriots owner Bob Kraft's reaction? Was he incensed and utterly embarrassed that Belichick would tarnish the name of his beloved Patriots? Was he beside himself with rage and indignation at the thought of fans everywhere doubting whether the Patriots were true Champions, or possibly frauds? Not exactly, his reaction was to award Bill Belichick with a six-year contract extension including a raise of more than $3 million per season.

On September 17, 2007, a week after the biggest cheating scandal the NFL had ever known, it was announced that the coach who was caught red-handed cheating had received a six-year extension and a raise from $4.5 to $7.5 million per season. [12] That ought to teach him!

SPYGATE

Endnotes

[1] Mortensen, Chris. "Sources: Goodell Determines Pats Broke Rules by Taping Jets' Signals." ESPN, September 13, 2007. http://sports.espn.go.com/nfl/news/story?id=3014677

[2] Sando, Mike. "What's Legal, What's Illegal in NFL Spy Game." ESPN, September 13, 2007. http://sports.espn.go.com/nfl/columns/story?columnist=sando_mike&id=3017542

[3] ESPN.com News Services. "Belichick Draws $500,000 Fine, But Avoids Suspension." ESPN, September 14, 2007. http://sports.espn.go.com/nfl/news/story?id=3018338

[4] ESPN.com News Services. "Belichick Issues Apology, Says He's Spoken with Goodell." ESPN, September 13, 2007. http://sports.espn.go.com/nfl/news/story?id=3015478

[5] National Football League. "NFL Rulebook." 2012. http://www.nfl.com/rulebook

[6] Branch, John and Greg Bishop. "New Claim of Taping Emerges Against Patriots." *The New York Times*, February 22, 2008. http://www.nytimes.com/2008/02/22/sports/football/22patriots.html?_r=2

[7] Gasper, Christopher L. "Specter Calls for Independent Investigation." Boston Globe, May 14, 2008. http://www.boston.com/sports/football/patriots/reiss_pieces/2008/05/specter_calls_f.html

[8] Belichick, Bill. "Eye to Eye: Bill Belichick," interview by Armen Keteyian, CBS News, September 20, 2007. http://www.youtube.com/watch?v=Hyg9BhqESxU

[9] Clayton, John. "Tape Runs Out on Patriots; Dungy Calls Incident 'Sad.'" ESPN.com, September 14, 2007. http://sports.espn.go.com/nfl/news/story?id=3019280

[10] U.S. Congress. Senate. Senator Arlen Specter of Pennsylvania speaking on New England Patriots Videotaping. 110th Cong., 2nd sess. *Congressional Record* (May 14, 2008), vol. 154, pt. 79:S4175–S4177.

[11] Fish, Mike. "Former Patriots Video Assistant Hints at Team's Spying History." ESPN, February 1, 2008. http://sports.espn.go.com/nfl/news/story?id=3226465

[12] Smith, Michael. "Sources: Patriots Give Belichick Long-Term Extension." ESPN, September 17, 2007. http://sports.espn.go.com/nfl/news/story?id=3023193

The NFL Cover-up

Chapter 2

The first thing every conspiracy buff knows: where there's smoke, there's fire. The smoke in this case was coming from the tapes that NFL commissioner Roger Goodell had literally set ablaze. After quickly viewing the incriminating tapes and notes collected from the New England Patriots, NFL officials burned all the evidence. For those scoring at home, when evidence is destroyed, antennas should go up. What most fans don't know is that the critical evidence of additional tapes and accompanying notes were destroyed at the scene of the crime in Foxboro, Massachusetts—not at the league offices in New York.[1] What could have been so damaging to the reputation of the National Football League that they could not allow the tapes to travel under armed guard to New York City?

This turn of events boggles the mind, and reeks of suspicion. Why destroy the tapes at all? What could possibly justify the NFL's destruction of key evidence in a case of national interest? If the tapes contained the signals of defensive coaches, as the

SPYGATE

NFL claimed, then why act so suspiciously? Sports fans were not alone in their suspicion. This destruction of evidence even got the attention of Senior Republican Pennsylvania Senator Arlen Specter. When Specter heard the explanations from Commissioner Goodell, he said, "The words 'absurd' and 'ridiculous' keep coming to mind because he [Goodell] says it with a straight face." [1]

NFL spokesman Greg Aiello confirmed that all documents and tapes were destroyed in Foxboro, Massachusetts, rather than in the league's New York offices. This occurred after they were reviewed by NFL officials Jeffrey Pash and Ray Anderson. Goodell himself gave the green light to destroy the material. Aiello stated, "There's no further use for it, so he [Goodell] said 'get rid of it.'" [1]

Conspiracy theorists worldwide would agree that there is no bigger indication of a cover-up than destroying evidence at the scene of a crime.

One must wonder how the NFL kept the media from exposing these glaringly obvious signs of a cover-up.

In a letter to NFL Commissioner Roger Goodell, Senator Specter wrote, "I am very concerned about the underlying facts of the taping, the reasons for the judgment of the limited penalties and most of all, on the inexplicable destruction of the tapes." [2]

An elder statesman, Senator Specter was no stranger to conspiracy theories. He had served as assistant counsel for the Warren Commission in 1963, a special commission established by President Lyndon Johnson to investigate the assassination of President John F. Kennedy. The public had become suspicious of a national-level cover-up of the JFK assassination. The Warren Commission was established so the public would feel confident the case was investigated fully. It was Senator Specter who helped devise the *single bullet theory*.

Goodell's explanation of why the NFL destroyed key evidence in a national scandal was awkward and dubious to say the least.

The Patriots had given the NFL six tapes, some from the 2007 season and the rest from the 2006 season. While Goodell said they were destroyed to prevent leaks to the media, one tape had already found its way to an analyst at Fox Sports, Jay Glazer. Glazer aired the footage, which showed clear shots of down and distance followed by coaches giving defensive signal gestures. The tape Glazer aired was the actual Patriots-Jets game that had ignited the controversy. "We wanted to take and destroy that information," Goodell said. "They may have collected it within the rules, but we couldn't determine that. So we felt that it should be destroyed." [2]

How does one collect signals "within the rules"? Vice President of NFL Operations Ray Anderson clarified the issue of stealing defensive signals in his memo in 2006, which specifically and flatly states that taping signals is never allowed. Someone was covering their tracks, and Goodell was clearly not adept at thinking on his feet.

No logical reason was ever given for destroying the evidence, not to mention the eyebrow-raising act of wiping out the evidence at Patriots team headquarters. How does anybody know what the tapes showed? Don't the other owners warrant the respect of getting to see firsthand exactly what the Patriots were up to? Apparently, whatever was on the tapes was enough to scare the hell out of Goodell. Perhaps if the public were to see the tapes, they would be convinced that the Patriots were not what they appear. Perhaps they would even question what it is that they watch on Sundays.

SPYGATE

The integrity of America's favorite pastime was in jeopardy. The league could not allow any of this to be considered, so they took a calculated risk and destroyed the evidence and ended up looking very suspicious in the process.

For his part, the good Senator was not going away. He was a Philadelphia man whose team had lost to the Patriots in Super Bowl XXXIX by only three points. He wanted to know if the cheating had helped the Patriots score those three points. He even said as much in a letter.

In a letter written January 31, 2008 from Goodell back to Specter (which the Senator released), Goodell stated that the tapes and notes in the investigation were destroyed to ensure that the Patriots "would not secure any possible competitive advantage as a result of the misconduct." [2]

Specter said the explanation "absolutely makes no sense at all." He also highly criticized the commissioner for not responding to the inquiries Specter had made into the matter over two months prior. His initial letter to the league was dated November 15, 2007, followed by another letter dated December 19, 2007. It was now two months since the original letter, with no response, and the Senator was losing his patience.

"There's a credibility issue here," Specter said. Clearly irritated, the Senator then tried some saber-rattling with a thinly-veiled threat. After all, Senator Specter had a lot of clout; he was the top Republican on the Senate Judiciary Committee. He warned that the questionable handling of this incident could put the NFL's antitrust exemption at risk. Specter stated, "Their antitrust exemption has been on my mind for a long time." [2]

The NFL operates under an antitrust exemption that allows it to exist as a virtual monopoly. It also allows the NFL to negotiate

TV rights with networks as one entity and not thirty-two separate organizations. Needless to say, it's worth a lot of money to the NFL. Arguing that sports are in the public interest, with special exemptions, Specter wanted answers.

"I don't think you have to have a law broken to have a legitimate interest by the Congress on the integrity of the game.... What if there was something on the tapes we might want to be subpoenaed, for example? You can't destroy it. That would be obstruction of justice," Specter said to the *New York Times*. [2]

Roger Goodell responded, "I am more than willing to speak with the Senator. There are very good explanations why the tapes were destroyed by our staff—there was no purpose for them." [2]

How could a person with his influence expect such a preposterous statement—that the tapes had no purpose—to be taken seriously?

Goodell claimed there was "no purpose" to retain key evidence in the biggest cheating scandal the NFL had ever known. Therefore, he immediately authorized destruction of all the evidence.

Specter was harshly critical of Goodell, saying that Goodell made "ridiculous" assertions that would not fly "in kindergarten." He continued, explaining that Goodell was caught in an "apparent conflict of interest," because the NFL did not want the public to lose confidence in the National Football League's integrity. [3]

Specter was more concerned about doing what was right:

"They are enormous role models for everybody," Specter said. "If you can cheat in the NFL, you can cheat in college, you can cheat in high school, you can cheat on your grade-school math test. There's no limit as to what you can do. I think they owe the public a lot more candor and a lot more credibility." [3]

SPYGATE

Likely revealing his true motives, Goodell wrote, "As the Commissioner and Competition Committee, we must take every appropriate step to safeguard the integrity of the NFL. We have already taken some positive and significant actions this past season, but we must go further to ensure fair competition amongst our thirty-two teams and maintain public confidence in our game." Goodell continued with this haltingly ironic statement: "Too often, competitive violations have gone unpunished because conclusive proof of the violation was lacking." [4]

This statement oozes hypocrisy. Goodell actually had conclusive proof of cheating—and he destroyed it on site.

What is so hard about a commissioner of a league dealing out punishment? Goodell disciplines his players without hesitation. As league commissioner, he usually does not need "conclusive proof" of anything. This is not a court of law, it's a league. In a league the commissioner is the law, is he not? This is surely easier to do when dealing with players; the commissioner has no allegiance to them and they have very little influence over his position or career (or salary). This dynamic becomes more complex when he is penalizing the owners, his bosses. Make no mistake, New England Patriots owner Robert Kraft is a very powerful and influential owner.

The truth was that Goodell was in a jam. He was in a fight for the very life of professional football as we know it. The potential repercussions were enormous, for a prominent franchise like the New England Patriots being found to actively employ a cheating system. Firstly, how could the commissioner disqualify a team and vacate one Super Bowl, much less three? A league official cannot just give the Lombardi Trophy to the team that lost in the Super Bowl game. Fans would not appreciate a team winning such a coveted award by default. What about the team that the Patriots had beaten in the AFC Championship game? Were there millions of dollars of contracts paid to players that achieved success "cheating"? Were the billions of dollars exchanged betting on these football games won or lost fraudulently? Should records and potential Hall of Fame achievements be reexamined? What of the millions of fans? Would they have cause to sue for damages? Did they pay to see legitimate games that were greatly influenced by the Spygate system? They have every right to see a game that is played honestly. Make no mistake; the domino effect caused by a pirated Super Bowl would be like a tsunami. It could literally bankrupt the NFL and cause their status as America's favorite sport to be swept out to sea, indefinitely lost.

This cheating scandal was far worse than the Black Sox scandal of 1919. The Chicago White Sox only cheated themselves; they conspired to actually lose a World Series, not win three Super Bowls.

Consider the millions of dollars in lost revenue from teams that were beaten soundly and regularly by an opponent that was not competing honestly. What about the businesses that cater to sports fans? Think about the bar owner with a location near the stadium or the vendor who sells T-shirts during playoff games. How about the coaches who were fired because their team was humiliated 52-6 in a game where cheating was involved?

Stories started coming fast and furiously. September 14, 2007: On ESPN Radio's *Mike & Mike Show*, Chris Mortensen reported the league might not close the book on the controversy, continuing to "review" it. Mortensen suggested that the videotaping of the September 9th game against the Jets could be the tip of the iceberg—that the Patriots' practices could include jamming the radio frequency in opponents' headsets, and wiring the Patriots' defensive linemen to eavesdrop on opposing quarterback audibles. [5]

This information was released by the media one day after the NFL brass had given its ruling and punishment. The case's hasty closing felt rushed and premature; shouldn't the league have fully investigated these claims and complaints, and waited for the results? It seemed as though they just wanted this messy situation cleaned up in a hurry.

Andrea Kremer of NBC reported that several teams might charge the Patriots with having stolen playbooks, and the convenient "malfunctioning" of visiting teams' headphones at both old Foxboro Stadium and the new Gillette Stadium. It is important to note these reported events only happened during the time Belichick was coach of the Patriots. [6]

It seemed that the other NFL teams had had enough of New England's Tom Clancy-style *Patriot Games*.

The following story was filed by the legendary *Sports Illustrated* NFL reporter Paul Zimmerman, aka Dr. Z.

A Detroit Lion told this story to Zimmerman:

> *"At one point we had a good drive going against the Patriots," said one Lion who wished to remain anonymous, but was willing to talk about the scandal. "Mike Martz [offensive coordinator for the Lions] really had 'em going. They [Patriots] were getting fouled up, lining up wrong; we were moving the ball. Then boom, the headset from the sidelines to the coaches' booth goes out. Next possession, we were moving the ball again and the same thing happened. You know, it only takes two or three plays to mess up a drive."* [7]

Matt Millen, the Lions' GM, said he was talking to another team's head coach at the league meetings in 2007. He told him this exact story.

> *"Yeah, I know," the other coach said. "Headset went out. It happened to me in Foxboro, too."* [7]

Two coaches, two different teams, same headset malfunction at a critical moment of the game—coincidence?

The biggest bombshell of all was the emergence of Matt Walsh. Walsh was an ex-Patriots employee, a videographer with the team during the 2000-2002 seasons—Belichick's first two seasons as head coach.

Word was spreading that he had more tapes in his possession, and that one of those tapes may be of the St. Louis Rams' walkthrough before they played the Patriots in Super Bowl XXXVI. A walkthrough is practice at half-speed, where a team will run though all of the plays they plan to use in an upcoming game. A tape of the Rams walkthrough would have given the Patriots an undeniably major advantage in that Super Bowl game.

Walsh was actually present at that Rams walkthrough; if he had a tape of a Super Bowl team practicing before the big game, it would be a crushing blow to the league's insistence that the tapes the Patriots were making had little effect on the outcome of games.

Everyone wanted to hear what Matt Walsh had to say: the media, the fans, and even Senator Arlen Specter. However, the NFL league office was in no hurry to get Matt Walsh's side of the story. His involvement became known in January of 2008. Walsh made it clear that he had information that was potentially damaging to the NFL, and wanted to come forward. However, Walsh claimed he was under a nondisclosure agreement that would put him in legal jeopardy with the Patriots, should he talk.

If the NFL wanted to hear from Matt Walsh, all they needed to do was give him unconditional immunity from prosecution. After all, if they really wanted the truth, they would not penalize a star witness. Anyone who watches *Law and Order* expects as much, never mind that no one had accused Walsh of any wrongdoing.

"Any objective or accurate reading of the correspondence would show that the NFL is trying to discourage Walsh from coming forward," Senator Specter told the *New York Times*. "Especially the requirement in the letter, where the NFL calls for the destruction of whatever Walsh turns over without any provision for me or anyone else to see it." [8] This destroying of new evidence point would soon be reversed by NFL attorneys.

As the months dragged on, the NFL would not offer unconditional immunity. NFL counsel Jeff Pash, the man who burned the original tapes, offered the following limited protection:

> "… This will confirm that, subject only to the limited conditions set forth below, neither the National Football League, nor the New England Patriots, nor any of their affiliates will initiate litigation or arbitration proceedings against Mr. Walsh for the truthful disclosure to Senator Specter or his staff or to the League of facts of which Mr. Walsh may have become aware while employed by the Patriots. This commitment extends to the disclosure of factual information that might otherwise be deemed confidential or a trade secret. In return, you have confirmed that Mr. Walsh will share with the League office the same information

that he shares with the Senator or his staff, and that he will do so at about the same time that he speaks with the Senator and/or his staff.

"The commitment is conditioned upon Mr. Walsh's promptly returning to the League Office, after he has been interviewed by Senator Specter or his staff, any and all documents or other items that he may have taken improperly from the Patriots during the period of his employment there, or which are otherwise the property of the Patriots, and his confirming, in writing, that all such documents or items have been returned.

"If Mr. Walsh's disclosures are truthful, the commitment not to initiate litigation or arbitration proceedings referred to above shall extend to the improper removal of any items that are returned." NFL spokesman Greg Aiello said, "We offer immunity from litigation under two conditions, that he is to tell the truth and he returns anything he took from the Patriots." [9]

The Patriots and the NFL wanted all of the tapes, and wanted to bind Mr. Walsh's testimony. Note the statement "If Mr. Walsh's disclosures are truthful…not to initiate litigation." They would not sue, if Walsh told the truth. Who would decide upon the truth? Certainly not the accused Patriots or the NFL in full cover-up mode. The entire purpose of his testimony was supposedly to uncover the truth about Spygate. It seems as if the NFL's only concern was containing the damage, not unearthing new facts the NFL might have preferred stayed buried.

The NFL not only wanted possession of the tapes, but they wanted assurances that more tapes would not surface in the future. This odd dance went unchallenged by everyone except Senator Specter. The story went largely uncovered.

> *"The NFL's proposal is not full indemnification,"* Walsh's attorney Michael Levy told ESPN. *"It is highly conditional and still leaves Mr. Walsh vulnerable. I have asked the NFL to provide Mr. Walsh with the necessary legal protections so that he can come forward with the truth without fear of retaliation or litigation. To best serve the interest of the public and everyone involved, I am hopeful the NFL will do so promptly."* [9]

Mr. Walsh's attorney suggested this language:

> *"The National Football League and any and all of its affiliates, on behalf of itself and the New England Patriots and any and all of its affiliates (the 'Patriots'), agrees to indemnify, defend and hold Mr. Walsh harmless from and against all losses, liabilities, damages, costs, fines, expenses, deficiencies, taxes, and reasonable fees and expenses of counsel and agents, including but not limited to any costs incurred responding to any investigation, inquiry, or proceeding or in the course of enforcement of this agreement, which may be sustained by Mr. Walsh…. Neither the League nor the Patriots will institute, maintain, prosecute, or authorize to be commenced any action or other proceeding against Mr. Walsh either in law or equity based in whole or in part upon any of the foregoing."* [9]

Translated to layman's terms, if Matt Walsh tells everything he knows, the NFL will leave him alone. Walsh's attorney didn't trust the NFL, and he had good reason. He had learned that an

NFL security officer (former FBI agent Dick Farley) had already interviewed two of Walsh's coworkers at a Cape Cod golf course.

"Sending a former FBI agent to investigate his professional and personal life has not left Mr. Walsh feeling confident that the National Football League simply wants to encourage him to come forward with whatever information he has," Levy said. [9]

These actions seem more focused on discrediting a witness rather than trying to find the truth. But why would the league want to discredit Walsh, before hearing what he had to say? Furthermore, why would the NFL clearly try to assist the Patriots' defense? One assumes that the idea is to get to the bottom of the scandal. Was the object of this investigation to shed light on the truth, or was it to suppress the truth?

Walsh had already expressed that his information was potentially damaging to the league as well as the Patriots' reputation as champions. Luckily for fans of the truth, the legal process slogged on for months; as Walsh was eager to speak, he started giving interviews.

> **Author's note: As of the writing of this book, no one has ever impugned or in any way shown Matt Walsh's comments to be false. He was never shown to have any reason to lie or embellish his story in any way.**

The owners, while not happy to learn they had a cheater in their midst, toed the company line. At league meetings in the spring of 2008, Robert Kraft delivered an apology to the other NFL owners in a closed session. Those in attendance stated that Kraft gave an impassioned and heartfelt speech. He expressed great remorse for his team's illegal filming practices and emphasized the kind of respect his family has for the league and the importance of being good partners. He stated emphatically how sorry he and his family were that his team had caused damage to the NFL and its brand. After this mea culpa Commissioner Roger Goodell gave a talk about the importance of the "integrity of the game." [10] No matter how infuriated the other owners may have been at Kraft, Belichick, and the Patriots, the commissioner reminded them to put a lid on it, lest they alarm the public about the true extent of the cheating system the Patriots had developed.

Jim Irsay, owner of the Indianapolis Colts stated, "We all have to realize we can be sitting on the other side of the chair. We're all human." Irsay continued his unjustifiable and astonishing comments: "To me, it's a past issue and it [the apology] wasn't necessary, but the fact they did it shows class." [11]

"We were all satisfied, every one of us," said John Mara, New York Giants President. "All of us have our different opinions about the Patriots, but we were all satisfied that this thing was investigated properly and that they came to the proper conclusion." [12] Note Mara's line, "All of us have our different opinions about the Patriots." Could Mara have implied that other owners are indeed upset with the Patriots?

Company man Bill Polian, president of the Indianapolis Colts, said of the Spygate incident, "It's behind all of us, it's time to move forward." [12]

Jets owner Woody Johnson said of Spygate: "It really has been solved." [11]

"The main thing is accountability from top to bottom in protecting integrity and maintaining the confidence of our fans," said Ray Anderson, NFL Vice President of football operations, and the man identified to have executed Goodell's order to burn the illegal tapes. "That's what we're looking for in terms of integrity and fair competition moving forward." Given his past behavior, these are unsettling words coming from the NFL's vice president of football operations. [13]

"I'm happy they did it," Broncos owner Pat Bowlen said. "I don't know they had to do it. But it was good to hear from them. We're all trying to move on from this thing. What was said will stay in the room, but it was good." [10]

Steelers chairman Dan Rooney issued a statement:

"We consider the tapes of our coaching staff during our games against the New England Patriots to be a non-issue. In our opinion, they had no impact on the results of those games…. The Steelers fully support the manner in which Commissioner Goodell handled the situation and the discipline that he levied against those who violated league rules." [14]

One unidentified owner said to the *New York Daily News*: "They paid the price for this. They want it to be over. We are all as strong as our weakest link and we spend a lot of time trying to protect the integrity of the game. We want to give the fans a fair game and a level playing field. You got to have a mea culpa, otherwise there is no chance to move forward." [15]

Observe the tone and words chosen by all of the owners and coaches, with an emphasis given on the integrity of the league.

The league's apparent intended message bears repeating: *Everything is fine, nothing to worry about folks. Let's all just drop the subject.*

In their collective agreement, the owners were closing ranks so quickly it looked like a drill at West Point. After all, if you had over one billion dollars of your family's net worth tied up in a National Football League franchise, and one of your partners

SPYGATE

had done something that could cause widespread disbelief in the authenticity of your product, you would likely do just as these owners did and repeat the company line. Winning trophies is great, but at the end of the day, owning a team in the National Football League is the mother of all cash cows with milk flowing like a fire hose.

The NFL owners had absolutely no idea exactly how far down the rabbit hole this surreal cheating scandal could take them. We know this with absolute certainty.

Firstly, the league had destroyed the tapes they had received from the Patriots, in Foxboro. This happened before the owners could view them—not even the commissioner got to see them. Secondly, the league had not yet interviewed Matt Walsh, nor viewed his tapes.

The quotes above occurred on or around April 1, 2008, after the owners' meetings. The NFL finally interviewed Matt Walsh on May 13th, one month later. Matt Walsh: the star witness, the videographer who was hired to tape and steal signals. Matt Walsh, the only known, non-current Patriots employee with firsthand knowledge of the Spygate system, had not yet been interviewed. The NFL finally interviewed Matt Walsh, the man who had in his possession several more illegal tapes, who was literally aching to talk about the scandal, on May 13, 2008.

How could the owners have known what Matt Walsh would say or what was on his tapes? The answer is simple: they did not care. They knew the Patriots had cheated, and they just wanted all the attention to go away. The NFL and the owners were covering up for the Patriots, and that cover-up continues to this day.

It seems as though some clever journalists should have picked up on this obvious timeline inconsistency regarding the "water under the bridge" attitude of Roger Goodell and NFL owners, when they had yet to interview Matt Walsh. The media had been oddly obedient with the NFL's desire to sweep this under the rug. Fortunately for fans of logic, the Associated Press Sports Editors did catch this glaring inconsistency. Below is a transcript of Roger Goodell being called out on his gaffe.

Author comments in brackets.

Roger Goodell: We're just waiting to talk to Matt Walsh, and we finally got an appointment on his schedule for May 13th. So we'll see him on May 13th and see what he has.

[Goodell seems to imply that Matt has been busy for four months—that he was the delay, not Goodell and NFL lawyers.]

Reporter: If you read the agreement about ten times, it sounds like you sort of know what Matt Walsh has?

[This "agreement" was the indemnification agreement that Walsh's attorneys asked for, so the Patriots would not be able to sue Walsh for disclosing information.]

Goodell: No, they've not been required nor have they provided us with anything that they have. We've read what you have read in the newspapers, and other individuals have said that he has evidence of walkthroughs and other things. We are anxious to see if that is the case, but we don't have any indication if [he] has or doesn't have.

SPYGATE

> **Reporter:** Why have you and other league officials said multiple times since Super Bowl week that you have done your investigation and that everything is already out there? Why did it take so long to come to an agreement with Walsh?

> *[Specifically, why say that the NFL is done investigating before speaking to Walsh?]*

> **Goodell:** You'll have to ask Mr. Levy that. He's the one who is asking for the restrictions. They have been the ones asking for protection, while everyone else we have spoken to never asked for any conditions. He was free to speak and he could have spoken any time.

> *[That is a patently false statement. The only thing Walsh and his attorneys asked for was full protection from the Patriots' lawyers, since Walsh was under a nondisclosure agreement. The NFL could have granted this protection in five minutes or less; it was the NFL who put all the stipulations on his ability to speak, as proven here. He was never "free to speak." It is clear that none of what the commissioner stated lined up with known facts.]*

The AP reporter catches Goodell further in his web of deceit:

> **Reporter:** What about the stipulation in the agreement that he not speak to any other third parties before he is interviewed with the NFL?

[*Didn't Goodell just say he was free to speak? What's going on here?*]

Goodell: That is because I would like to see what he has. As soon as I am done here I am walking out to a media press conference, and anything he has he can tell you.

Reporter: Why is it important that you know first?

[*Why, indeed?*]

Goodell: Because it is a violation of NFL rules. If what you reported is correct, that he has a walkthrough, then I want to see that. If he has that, then I will be the first to be out there telling you. [16]

[*Given Goodell's past behavior, he was as likely to destroy the tape as he was of sharing its contents with a reporter.*]

Kudos to the fine folks at the Associated Press for their singular effort to actually shed light on this masquerade of an investigation, which they successfully showed in all of its absurdity. As mentioned earlier, Goodell is not a skilled bender of truth. He probably never needed to lie like this before in his life.

The Matt Walsh interviews will be discussed later, but first, let's meet some of the important players in this fascinating mystery.

SPYGATE

Endnotes

[1] Fish, Mike. "Specter: Goodell's Spygate Explanations Don't Pass Scrutiny." ESPN, February 15, 2008. http://sports.espn.go.com/nfl/news/story?id=3246788

[2] Fish, Mike. "Senator Wants to Know Why NFL Destroyed Patriots Spy Tapes." ESPN, February 2, 2008. http://sports.espn.go.com/nfl/news/story?id=3225539

[3] ESPN.com News Services. "Specter Criticizes NFL, Wants Independent Spygate Investigation." ESPN, May 15, 2008. http://sports.espn.go.com/nfl/news/story?id=3395829

[4] ESPN.com News Services. "Goodell Proposes Plan Making Cheating Penalties Easier to Impose." ESPN, March 7, 2008. http://sports.espn.go.com/nfl/news/story?id=3280996

[5] ESPN.com. "Timeline of Events and Disclosures During Spygate Saga." ESPN, May 12, 2008. http://sports.espn.go.com/nfl/news/story?id=3392047

[6] Easterbrook, Gregg. "Belichick's Cheating Could Lead to Dark Days for NFL." ESPN, October 10, 2007. http://sports.espn.go.com/espn/page2/story?page=easterbrook/070918

[7] Zimmerman, Paul. "Smooth Criminals: Patriots Bring Cheating in the NFL into Modern Era." *Sports Illustrated*, September 13, 2007. http://sportsillustrated.cnn.com/2007/writers/dr_z/09/13/cheating/index.html

[8] Bishop, Greg. "Specter Raises New Questions on Spying." *The New York Times*, March 9, 2008. http://www.nytimes.com/2008/03/09/sports/football/09nfl.html

[9] Fish, Mike. "Walsh's Attorney Says NFL Indemnification Offer Falls Short." ESPN, February 15, 2008. http://sports.espn.go.com/nfl/news/story?id=3248267

[10] Clayton, John "Kraft, Belichick Address Owners, Apologize for Spygate." ESPN, April 1, 2008. http://sports.espn.go.com/nfl/news/story?id=3323437

[11] "NFL Owners Meetings: Kraft Apologizes For Spygate Scandal." *Sports Business Journal Daily*, April 2, 2008. http://www.sportsbusinessdaily.com/Daily/Issues/2008/04/Issue-133/Leagues-Governing-Bodies/NFL-Owners-Meetings-Kraft-Apologizes-For-Spygate-Scandal.aspx

[12] Branch, John and Greg Bishop. "New Claim of Taping Emerges Against Patriots." *The New York Times*, February 22, 2008. http://www.nytimes.com/2008/02/22/sports/football/22patriots.html?_r=2

SPYGATE

[13] Clayton, John. "Goodell Could Get Another Tool to Defend Sport." ESPN, March 18, 2008. http://sports.espn.go.com/nfl/columns/story?columnist=clayton_john&id=3320938

[14] Harris, John. "Rooney: Spygate 'Had No Impact' in Losses to Patriots." *Tribune-Review*, February 15, 2008. http://www.pittsburghlive.com/x/pittsburghtrib/s_552617.html

[15] Daily News Staff Writer. "Robert Kraft Apologizes for SpyGate; Bill Belichick Misinterpreted Rule." *New York Daily News*, April 2, 2008. http://articles.nydailynews.com/2008-04-02/sports/17895302_1_defensive-signals-bill-belichick-questions-so-many-times

[16] Monkovic, Toni. "Rodger Goodell Interview Transcript." *The New York Times*, May 1, 2008. http://fifthdown.blogs.nytimes.com/2008/05/01/roger-goodell-transcript/

The Players

Section II

Tom Brady

Chapter 3

Thomas Edward Patrick Brady, Jr. was born on August 3, 1977 in San Mateo, California. Being from the San Francisco area, he grew up a 49ers fan. As a child, Brady idolized Joe Montana and attended many 49ers games in the 1980s. Brady was in attendance when Dwight Clark made "The Catch" at the 1981 NFC Championship game.

Brady attended Junipero Serra High School in San Mateo, where he was a multi-sport athlete. During his high school football career he completed 236 of 447 passes (a 53% rate) for 3,514 yards, with 33 touchdowns. He was also an exceptional baseball player. Brady was an all-star catcher who was drafted by the Montreal Expos in the 18th round of the 1995 Major League Baseball Draft.[1] For Brady, baseball was an offseason diversion; his real love was football.

Thus he chose to pursue his football career as a scholarship player at the University of Michigan. During his first two years as a Michigan Wolverine, he was on the bench as a backup quarterback, an understudy. The starting quarterback at the time was Brian Griese, son of NFL Hall of Fame quarterback Bob Griese. Brian Griese led the Wolverines to a share of the national championship in 1997 while winning the Rose Bowl. Playing in Griese's shadow was hard on young Brady; although Griese was clearly the starter, Brady was frustrated by his lack of playing time. This became such an issue that he even briefly considered transferring to the University of California.

He eventually became the Michigan starting quarterback in his sophomore year of eligibility. The team had a very good year with Brady as the starter that season. Brady led the team to a 10-3 record and won the Citrus Bowl over Arkansas in 1998, to cap off the season. The following year the Wolverines landed one of the most highly recruited athletes in the country, quarterback Drew Henson. A baseball and football star that had been drafted by the New York Yankees, Henson was dubbed the *Golden Boy* by *Sports Illustrated*. [2] In Henson's freshman year, head coach Lloyd Carr started rotating Brady and Henson during games in an effort to get Henson some playing time. As Henson was his quarterback of the future, Carr was bowing to public pressure.

All the fans wanted to see Henson in action. Carr was also acutely aware that millions of dollars awaited Henson if he suddenly decided to bolt to the New York Yankees and a Major League Baseball career.

When the coach asked Henson to enter a game to relieve Brady, the Michigan fans erupted in cheers. [3] This was clearly a very difficult time in Brady's life. In spite of Henson's *Golden Boy* shadow, in the last game of the 1999 season, Brady ended his college career with a spectacular performance. In the Orange Bowl win over Alabama, Brady threw for 369 yards and 4 touchdowns.

Brady was ready to turn pro. He had played well enough, but still had Drew Henson breathing down his neck most of his senior year. Henson had played in nine games Brady's senior year as Coach Carr played musical chairs at quarterback, trying to keep Henson from leaving Michigan to play baseball for the Yankees.

When Brady entered the 2000 NFL draft he assumed that he had a great shot at being drafted. After all, he had won 20 of 25 games as a starter. He was tall at 6'4", showed good arm strength, and displayed superb accuracy. Brady expected that if things went as planned, he would be drafted in the middle rounds. [3]

Unfortunately for Brady, the NFL scouts did not agree with his self-assessment. Although there are at least two pre-draft scouting reports on Brady, this report will list the common threads. Everything here is written by scouts:

> Tom Brady Positives: *Good height to see the field. Very poised and composed. Smart, can read coverages. Good accuracy and touch. A pocket-type passer who plays well in big spots and in big games, he is a gamer. Team leader will do well as a system-type quarterback.*

Sounds like the Tom Brady fans know, right?

> Tom Brady Negatives: *Poor build, very skinny and narrow. Ended the 99 season 6' 4" and 195 lbs, still looks like a rail at 211. Looks a little frail and lacks great physical stature and strength. Can get easily pushed down. Lacks mobility (40 yard dash in 5.28 seconds) and can't avoid a rush. Lacks a really strong arm. Can't drive the ball down field and does not throw*

a really tight spiral. System-type player who can get exposed if he must ad-lib and do things on his own.

Summary: *Is not what you're looking for in terms of physical stature, strength, arm strength, and mobility, but he has the intangibles and production, and showed great Griese-like improvement as a senior. Could make it in the right system but will not be for everyone.*

From these scouting reports, Tom Brady was rightfully not on many draft boards. Much to Tom's dismay, he was finally selected in the sixth round by New England, pick #199.

It is easy to see why Brady lasted until the sixth round on draft day. The other teams did not exactly make a scouting error by not drafting Brady. He actually was statue-slow and rail-thin. Regardless of his win/loss record in college, he looked like he might last one week in an NFL training camp before being crushed by a linebacker. NFL defenders are cat-quick and extremely powerful. A quarterback with no build and slow feet is likely to have a bleak fate in the lightning-fast NFL.

His recent past had shown that Brady was forced to share playing time at quarterback with a freshman at Michigan. He was not even the clear-cut starter on an above-average Michigan team. Most damaging was the observation that his arm was good but not exceptional. In point of fact, the Patriots did not spot a gem in Tom Brady. If that was the case, they would have drafted him in the fourth or fifth round. New England took a flyer on a quarterback that showed he was a winner and a "gamer" with a sixth round pick, essentially a throw-away pick.

To say the Patriots were handsomely rewarded is to state the obvious. It is interesting that the scouts observed him as a system-type quarterback, as though that could be good or bad depending on the team that drafted him. Most of their reporting was correct. Tom Brady is not a Brett Favre gunslinger type of quarterback. When he is hit or pressured he does not play well. He currently plays for a team in New England with an elaborate system, and in that system Brady has no equal. Regarding his arm, however, they were dead wrong. Brady throws a perfect spiral and has little problem making any throw on the field. Tom Brady is a top flight NFL quarterback by nearly every measure.

Brady made the roster, which is not a guarantee for a sixth-rounder. For the 2000 season he was listed as the fourth quarterback on the depth chart. Not many teams will carry four quarterbacks; Brady was on the cusp of not making the team.

By the end of the 2000 season he had worked his way up to #2 on the depth chart. He was now the backup to three-time Pro Bowler, Drew Bledsoe.

Brady's big break came during the second game of the 2001 season against the Jets. Drew Bledsoe was hit so hard that he sheared a blood vessel in his chest. The injury was so serious that Bledsoe suffered from internal bleeding. Bledsoe would be lost for months.

Tom Brady replaced Bledsoe in that game and the Patriots lost the game to the Jets 10-3. This loss made the Patriots' record 0-2, placing them last in their division. Then suddenly the Patriots started hitting on all cylinders. All the breaks started to go their way; Brady was proficient beyond his years. He won eleven of the fourteen games he started, including six in a row, a rarely seen feat for a young quarterback in his first NFL season.

After winning the AFC East and the #2 seed, they met the Oakland Raiders in Foxboro in the divisional round. In that game Brady threw for 312 yards and led the Patriots back from a ten-point fourth quarter deficit. The Patriots won this game in overtime on an Adam Vinatieri field goal. This was the famous "tuck rule" game in which Brady clearly fumbled after being hit by former fellow Michigan Wolverine, Charles Woodson. The referees ruled "incomplete pass" based on an obscure rule called the "tuck rule." This ruling saved the game for New England.

The rule itself reads:

> **NFL Rule 3, Section 22, Article 2, Note 2.** *When [an offensive] player is holding the ball to pass it forward, any intentional forward movement of his arm starts a forward pass, even if the player loses possession of the ball as he is attempting to tuck it back toward his body. Also, if the player has tucked the ball into his body and then loses possession, it is a fumble.* [4]

The road to the Super Bowl led through Pittsburgh and the AFC Championship Game versus the #1 seed Pittsburgh Steelers. Nearing the end of the first half, Tom Brady was injured and had to leave the game—he would not return. His backup Drew Bledsoe replaced him in the lineup. The Patriots did not miss a beat in Tom's absence. The Patriots moved the ball efficiently against the NFL's top defense, almost as though it did not matter who their quarterback was that day. The Patriots won the game 24-17. They were immediately set as 14-point underdogs against the high-flying St. Louis Rams in Super Bowl XXXIV.

At that time, the Rams were commonly known as the *Greatest Show on Turf* and that particular Super Bowl was to be played at the Louisiana Superdome...on turf.

In Super Bowl XXXIV, Kurt Warner's Rams were not nearly as effective on offense as they had been all year long. Warner was having a dream season up until that game. The Rams typically displayed an explosive offense. During the regular season they had scored 503 points, an eye-popping 31 points per game. But on this day, through three quarters they only managed 3 points. The Rams had previously played the Patriots, in Foxboro, earlier in that season. In that game, St. Louis scored 24 points in a 7-point win over the Patriots. But in this game, things were different.

Once again, in Super Bowl XXXVI Brady proved cool beyond his years. The Patriots won this game in dramatic fashion, winning 20-17 on a game-winning field goal from 48 yards out. Brady's stat line was efficient 16 of 27 for 145 yards, and one touchdown with no interceptions. He was named Super Bowl MVP and became the youngest Super Bowl-winning quarterback in NFL history.

In his first year as an NFL starter, Brady had a very low interception total of 12. Here is a short list of Hall of Fame Quarterbacks' touchdowns and interceptions for their first full year starting in the NFL. [5]

	TDs	INTs
Troy Aikman	9	18
John Elway	7	14
Peyton Manning	26	28
Brett Favre	19	24
Jim Kelly	22	17
Terry Bradshaw	13	22
Tom Brady	**18**	**12**

In the past fifteen years, the Super Bowl winning quarterback has always been a player who was highly rated coming out of college. In the era of the 24/7 information age it should be nearly impossible to miss an extremely talented quarterback whose performance could lead to hundreds of millions of dollars in revenue for the lucky NFL owner who can pick a winner on draft day.

Not surprisingly, nearly every individual Super Bowl-winning quarterback in the last fifteen years (except Brady) was drafted in the first or second round. Brady is widely regarded as the prime example that a Super Bowl-winning quarterback can be found anywhere in the draft. However, that is simply not the case.

Take a look at the last fifteen Super Bowl winners and the round in which they were drafted: [5]

Super Bowl XXX	Troy Aikman	Round 1
Super Bowl XXXI	Brett Favre	Round 2
Super Bowl XXXII	John Elway	Round 1
Super Bowl XXXIII	John Elway	Round 1
Super Bowl XXXIV	Kurt Warner	Undrafted
Super Bowl XXXV	Trent Dilfer	Round 1
Super Bowl XXXVI	Tom Brady	Round 6
Super Bowl XXXVII	Brad Johnson	Round 9
Super Bowl XXXVIII	Tom Brady	Round 6
Super Bowl XXXIX	Tom Brady	Round 6
Super Bowl XL	Ben Roethlisberger	Round 1
Super Bowl XLI	Peyton Manning	Round 1
Super Bowl XLII	Eli Manning	Round 1
Super Bowl XLIII	Ben Roethlisberger	Round 1
Super Bowl XLIV	Drew Brees	Round 2
Super Bowl XLV	Aaron Rodgers	Round 1

While Kurt Warner did not get drafted at all, he made it to an NFL camp in 1994 with the Green Bay Packers. He was soon cut because, as scouts suspected, he was not a suitable NFL quarterback, having started only one year at lowly Northern Iowa University. Warner then played four years professionally in the Arena Football League and NFL Europe where he developed the uncanny ability to throw a football virtually through the eye of a needle. Kurt Warner was 28 years old when he finally entered the NFL and began his magical ride. His undrafted status was understandable and correct, given his level of play at that time.

Brad Johnson was drafted in the ninth round in 1992, and he won his Super Bowl at the relatively ripe age of 34, when most quarterbacks are retiring. He had been in the league for over ten years when he won the big game.

The point being, there is absolutely no precedent for a player who fell into the late rounds of a modern draft and then winning a Super Bowl in his first year of NFL action. Tom Brady is an extreme outlier in this respect. Professional scouts sometimes overrate college quarterback prospects. With 32 teams drafting and everyone needing a quarterback, a lower rated college quarterback coming into the NFL and breaking records, then winning a Super Bowl in his first year of NFL play simply does not happen.

Brady would go on to become the only quarterback to win three Super Bowls in four years. Winning multiple championships is an amazing accomplishment given the parity and highly competitive nature of the NFL.

In Super Bowl XXXVIII Brady was the MVP of the game. The Patriots won a close game by the score of 32-29. His stat line for that game: he completed 32 of 48 passes (67%) for 354 yards, 3 touchdowns with 1 interception.

In Super Bowl XXXIX the Patriots beat the Philadelphia Eagles 24-21 in another game that went down to the wire. Brady's stat

SPYGATE

line for this Super Bowl: he completed 23 of 33 passes (70%) for 236 yards, 2 touchdowns with zero interceptions.

Here is partial list of the NFL records Tom Brady holds:

Most touchdown passes in a single regular season (50)
Highest touchdown to interception ratio in a season (9:1)
Highest single-game completion percentage 26/28 (93%)
Highest winning percentage for his first 100 starts as a quarterback (76)
First quarterback to throw 200 career passing touchdowns with fewer than 100 interceptions (88)
Longest streak of consecutive passing attempts without an interception (335)
Most consecutive games won (21)
Most passing touchdowns in a quarter (5)
Most games with 4 touchdowns and zero interceptions (12)
Highest completion to interception ratio (81-1)

How much did the Patriots' system of taping opponents and otherwise eavesdropping on privileged information help Tom Brady and the Patriots achieve these accomplishments? That is difficult to determine. The system the Patriots use has always been touted by Belichick as one in which the team is more important than the individual players. But surely Tom Brady is irreplaceable; observe all that he has accomplished from the very beginning of his NFL career. He could be dubbed a "once in a lifetime" quarterback. Is it possible that the system "makes" Tom Brady, and not the other way around? If only there was a way to test this theory.

Enter, Matt Cassel. In 2008 Tom Brady had a season-ending injury in the opening game of the season. Matt Cassel, who had last started a football game at Chatsworth High School in California, replaced Brady in the lineup.

Matt Cassel currently holds an unusual NFL record that will likely never be broken. In the last 40 years of NFL play, he is believed to be the only quarterback to have started an NFL game without ever starting a single college game as quarterback. Cassel, a seventh round draft choice, was drafted out of the University of Southern California. He had been the backup to Heisman Trophy winners Carson Palmer and Matt Leinart. With no college football experience as a springboard, 26-year-old Matt Cassel amazed the football world by leading the team to an 11-5 record. He even looked eerily similar to Tom Brady in his poise and playing style.

Consider the stat lines below. Each represents a stat line of two different seasons of NFL quarterback play. See if you can guess which line is Brady's first year as an NFL starter, and which line is Cassel's first year starting, since high school five years prior.

TDs	Interceptions	Completion %	Yards Passing
18	12	64	2,843
21	11	63	3,693

According to these statistics, it does not seem to matter who plays quarterback in New England. With three more touchdowns, one less interception, and 850 more yards passing, the clear winner is actually Matt Cassel. These are the published stat lines from Tom Brady's 2001 Super Bowl year and Matt Cassel's 2008 seasons, respectively. [5]

Furthermore, in an even more direct indication of Brady's relative value to the Patriots, Brady has been consistently and

SPYGATE

conspicuously underpaid by the New England Patriots nearly his entire career. This data point will be expanded upon in a later chapter.

Bill Belichick appeared on ESPN's *Mike & Mike* radio show in December of 2011. He was asked "How great is Tom Brady?" by host Mike Greenberg. Belichick said, "He's a hard worker...he's very well prepared...I am glad he is our quarterback. But I am also proud of the fact that without Tom Brady, we still won 11 games in 2008." [6] Belichick might be the only coach who would marginalize a three-time Super Bowl-winning quarterback that way. Winning football is all about his system in Belichick's mind. He may indeed be correct.

Has any other quarterback come off the bench due to the injury of a starting quarterback, and proceeded to lead his team to a Super Bowl title? Yes, actually. Jeff Hostetler led the New York Giants, a big underdog, to an improbable win over the Buffalo Bills, led by Jim Kelly, in Super Bowl XXV. Hostetler had replaced Phil Simms, who had broken his foot late in the season. Coaching the defense for the Giants in that Super Bowl was none other than Bill Belichick. Sometimes truth really is stranger than fiction.

Endnotes

[1] Junipero Serra High School. "2004 Athletic Hall of Fame Inductees." 2010. http://www.serrahs.com/page.cfm?p=2552

[2] Montville, Leigh. "Golden Boy." *Sports Illustrated*, August 3, 1998. http://sportsillustrated.cnn.com/vault/article/magazine/MAG1013468/index.htm

[3] Halberstam, David. *The Education of a Coach*. New York: Hyperion, 2005.

[4] National Football League. "NFL Rulebook." 2012. http://www.nfl.com/rulebook

[5] Pro-Football-Reference.com. "Pro Football Statistics and History." 2012. http://www.pro-football-reference.com/

[6] Belichick, Bill. Interview by Mike Greenberg and Mike Golic, in "Mike and Mike in the Morning." *ESPN Boston Radio*, December 2, 2011.

Bill Belichick:
A Coaching Legend is Born

Chapter 4

Bill Belichick is a complex and enigmatic individual. He was raised in Annapolis, Maryland, the son of a US Naval Academy football coach and scout. Steve Belichick, his father, began speaking the X's and O's of football strategy to his son from a very early age. They were breaking down film together since Bill was knee high. Bred to be a coach, young Bill learned the discipline it takes to spend hours breaking down game film. It was like searching for buried treasure, the secrets that other teams possessed. Secrets that, if mastered, could help your team win a football game. The way a team lined up could tip you off to what play they might run. If studied, a team may show certain tendencies you could identify.

Bill played football and loved it, but he was not an exceptional player. He lacked the build and speed commonly associated with star players. However, his knowledge of the game helped him play beyond the level of his physical ability. After graduating from high school he enrolled at Phillips Academy in Andover,

Massachusetts for one postgraduate year. The reason being, he needed to improve his grades in order to gain entry into a quality university. It was at Phillips Academy that he would meet Ernie Adams, a kindred spirit with a keen mind. Oddly, Adams was also born to be a football coach. Belichick and Adams began a friendship that would last forty years, and continues to this day. After Andover, Belichick enrolled at Wesleyan University in Middletown, Connecticut. At Wesleyan he played center and tight end on the football team. He also played squash and lacrosse, serving as the captain of the lacrosse team his senior year. Upon graduation he was eager to begin his lifelong dream of becoming a coach. The year was 1975. [1]

His father made a few calls on his son's behalf; as a well-known coach in the New England area himself, he had many contacts in the coaching community. Bill's first coaching position was a $25-a-week stint as an assistant for the Baltimore Colts, under head coach Ted Marchibroda. The job began as an unpaid assistant and utilized Bill's proficiency of breaking down game film. He was so talented that the Colts eventually started paying him for his excellent work. The following year he joined the Detroit Lions as an assistant special teams coach. He was exceptionally skilled at film work—in those days, so few people had mastered this increasingly important skill. However, he also seemed to rub many players the wrong way. In his book *The Education of a Coach*, author David Halberstam writes that even in Belichick's first jobs, with no reputation to back him up, he was cocky and brash. The players referred to him as "The Punk" and wanted to "clock him". [1] The author even forebodingly stated that Belichick was good at picking up on players' "tells." A tell is a sign, a posture or foot position, that might indicate a player's intentions. "It was like having a great spy working for us," Halberstam relates. [1]

In 1978 he moved again, this time to Denver with a job his prep school friend Ernie Adams helped procure. Once again, Bill was breaking down game film specifically for defensive coach Joe Collier. It was while he was in Denver with coach Richie McCabe that Belichick learned the Al Davis coaching system. McCabe had been a coach in Oakland for a few years and passed on the knowledge he picked up from Davis. Tips included how to use other teams' discarded players, and the process of continuously grading and evaluating players, even after you had acquired them. Bill learned that keeping players in line was critical at the professional level.

In 1979 Bill got his big break. Ernie Adams had gained the ear and trust of Giants head coach Ray Perkins. One interview later, Belichick the nomad had finally landed a real coaching gig with a real paycheck. He was named the Special Teams Coach and added Linebackers Coach to his responsibilities in 1980. By 1985 he was the Defensive Coordinator of the Giants under Bill Parcells. It is not at all clear what Ernie Adams' duties were at the Giants complex, but the important point is that the boyhood friends were together at last in the NFL. Their lifelong dream of coaching together at the professional level had become reality.

In 1986 the Giants had a regular season record of 14-2 and rolled into Super Bowl XXI. It was during this season the Giants players popularized the practice of giving a winning coach a "Gatorade Shower." The Giants were victorious in Super Bowl XXI due to a scintillating performance by Phil Simms. His record setting 88% pass completion rate, and the Giants "Big Blue Wrecking Crew" defense, was too much for the Denver Broncos.

SPYGATE

The Giants scored 30 second half points to win 39-20. This 1986 Giants team is referred to by many in the sports media as one of the greatest NFL teams of all time.

Belichick was only 34 at the time, and his coaching star was on the rise. Belichick would return to the Super Bowl a few years later, after the 1990 season. In Super Bowl XXV, the Giants faced the Buffalo Bills, led by Jim Kelly. The heavily favored Bills featured the NFL's top scoring offense, with 428 points scored that year (26 per game). Conversely, the Giants had the stingiest defense, allowing only 211 points scored (13 per game) against them. The Giants shocked America by winning the closest Super Bowl ever played, by one point. The final score was Giants 20, Bills 19. That Super Bowl game became known as the "wide right" game after Bills kicker Scott Norwood missed the late game field goal from 47 yards out.

However, in football circles, it was Belichick that got all the credit. His defensive game plan for Super Bowl XXV is currently on display at the Pro Football Hall of Fame in Canton, Ohio. To be candid, Bill Parcells loaded the Giants team on the defensive side by design. Through superior drafting they acquired some of the most fearsome linebackers in the NFL. They had Lawrence Taylor, Carl Banks, and Pepper Johnson in the prime of their careers. The Giants were a sound team, but it was their defense that dominated.

After this impressive season Bill Parcells "retired." Belichick was a hot young coach on everybody's short list of head coaching candidates. Some were calling Belichick a defensive genius. Parcells' bigger-than-life personality, coupled with his "one voice" philosophy, had allowed Belichick to hide his most obvious weakness: his "not ready for prime time" personality. He was introverted and lacked the charisma most head coaches view as an essential trait in their position.

Nonetheless, Belichick was offered and accepted the head coach position with the Cleveland Browns. He accepted the job and contacted his old pal Ernie Adams. He was happy to finally be out from under Parcells' enormous shadow. Ernie Adams had taken a hiatus from football and was working on Wall Street when he got the call. With Belichick becoming a head coach in the NFL, it was time to get back to the game he loved.

The Cleveland Browns from 1991 to 1995 were not the Cleveland Browns we know and love today. They were not the Al Lerner *Bad News Browns*. These Browns were the Art Modell Browns. The Browns' record in the five years prior to Belichick's arrival was impressive, to say the least. It's easy to look at the recent struggles of the Browns and think, "Of course Belichick didn't succeed in Cleveland—nobody wins in Cleveland." In the early 1990s, this would be wholly inaccurate. Remember, these Browns moved in 1995 to become the Baltimore Ravens. The Browns in 1991 were an excellent football team.

In his first head coaching opportunity, Bill Belichick made some very big mistakes, by his own admission. He was rude and rough with the media, a tactic he had inappropriately learned from Bill Parcells. Parcells had gotten away with his brashness for two reasons:

1. Parcells was actually humorous with his acerbic quips, directed at media members or players. He had a wide smile, was a big man physically, and was very charismatic. In person, Belichick was the antithesis of Parcells.

2. Parcells was a winner. Parcells did not start out as a brute with the media and his players. He evolved into that persona after he started winning. Belichick had not earned his stripes yet in Cleveland, and still he brazenly started off his new job by rubbing everyone the wrong way. He was mimicking Parcells' style and people around him resented it. [1]

Shortly into his tenure, both the Cleveland players and the media strongly disliked Belichick. Parcells' players played hard for him, even if they disliked him, because they knew if they bought into the Parcells' system, they would become winners. The Cleveland players had no reason to give their new coach the benefit of that doubt. Belichick had no charm or wit about him, and most damagingly, he was not winning. Known as a defensive genius, Belichick's Browns' defenses were middle-of-the-pack in terms of points allowed rankings. To make matters worse, Belichick unceremoniously benched Cleveland's favorite son, quarterback Bernie Kosar. Kosar was a local product from Youngstown, Ohio, and had been a very good starting quarterback for the Browns. He was a proven clutch player who had been extremely successful in his first five years in Cleveland. He was so beloved, if Kosar had run for Mayor of Cleveland, he might have won. [1]

It is popular NFL mythology that Belichick inherited a sorry Cleveland Browns team. The myth places the fault in Cleveland, and somehow not on Belichick—but myths are not always true. Look back at the team Belichick inherited when he took over in 1991.

Bernie Kosar's rookie year was 1985. Although he had only gotten the nod as starter in midseason, he immediately proved he belonged in the NFL. Kosar was assisted by two great running backs, Earnest Byner and Kevin Mack; each of these young studs rushed for over 1,000 yards that season. The Browns won the AFC Central with an 8-8 record. They looked to be the spoiler in the divisional round of the playoffs when they took a 21-3 lead into the second half against the heavily favored Miami Dolphins. Quarterback Dan Marino did, in fact, lead a second half comeback to win the game 24-21, ending the Browns' surprising season. However, hopes were high in Cleveland—they had a legit NFL franchise quarterback, the best running back tandem in the NFL, and a defense that was coming into its own. In addition, they had hot young coach, Marty Schottenheimer.

The 1986 season saw the Browns break into NFL elite status. They finished 12-4 behind Bernie Kosar's 3,854 yards, with one of the NFL's stingiest defenses. The defense featured five Pro Bowlers and earned the AFC's top seed. The Browns beat the New York Jets in the divisional round 23-20 in double overtime. The 1986 AFC Championship was an all-time classic game, matching the up-and-coming Denver Broncos with new powerhouse Cleveland Browns. This game is famous for the way John Elway led his team back from 7 points down with 5:11 left in the game. Starting on his own two yard line, he drove 98 yards, throwing the tying touchdown pass with only 34 seconds left in the game. This event is known in football lore as "The Drive" and the beginning of Elway's legend. The Broncos won in overtime, sending them to the Super Bowl.

The Browns' success continued in 1987 with Kosar again passing for over 3,000 yards. They won the AFC Central with a record of 10-5 and pounded the Indianapolis Colts 38-20 in the divisional round of playoffs. Once again, they would meet Elway and the Broncos in the AFC Championship Game, this time in

SPYGATE

Denver. Although the Broncos ran out to a 21-3 halftime lead, Kosar showed his steel by engineering a comeback, and tied the game 31-31 in the fourth quarter. This game should have ended in a Super Bowl berth for the Browns, if not for "The Fumble."

The winning touchdown was a few short yards away from Browns running back Ernest Byner, when suddenly Broncos defensive back Jeremiah Castille miraculously stripped him of the ball. Another shocking loss to the Broncos kept them from advancing to the Super Bowl. Another heartbreaking loss for Browns fans.

In 1988 the Browns finished 10-6, even though Kosar and two of his backups were injured during the season. Even with backups starting at quarterback, Schottenheimer got the Browns into the playoffs only to lose to the Oilers in the opening round. To be sure, the Browns were a major football power in the late 1980s. Schottenheimer's teams, with Kosar at quarterback, had reached the playoffs each of their five seasons together, advancing to the AFC Championship Game in three of those years. Schottenheimer and the Browns mutually agreed to split after the 1988 season, but not because the team lacked quality. Modell thought his team was very close to a Super Bowl Championship and was looking for someone to get them over the hump. He was sick of losing close games deep into the playoffs.

The 1989 Browns under first-year head coach Bud Carson opened the season by demolishing the Pittsburgh Steelers 51-0 at Three Rivers Stadium. This game was the all-time worst loss in Steelers history. The Browns of the late 1980s were a team to be reckoned with. Once again, they made it back to the AFC Championship, and again, lost to their archrival, the Broncos.

In 1990, the team sputtered and Carson was fired after nine games. This is the team that hired Belichick as their head coach in 1991. How do these events square with the story told by Belichick and Adams, as relayed to author David Halberstam in *The Education of a Coach*? [1] In the boyhood friends' collective alternate version of reality, the Browns were an old team with no good players. They tell a tale where Belichick had no chance at success, with the media and owner all lined up against him. In truth, Belichick benched Bernie Kosar, a hometown hero, effectively ruining what could have been a Hall of Fame career. Belichick's failure in Cleveland led to one of the NFL's proudest franchises leaving town under cover of darkness. That football team became the Baltimore Ravens. The Ravens soon resumed their winning ways, and finally won the Super Bowl in 2000 under Brian Billick.

After amassing a 36 win, 44 loss record in five seasons as head coach of the Cleveland Browns, Belichick was fired at the end of the 1995 season. With the team moving to Baltimore, a clean start was best for all parties. During Belichick's difficult years in Cleveland, all he heard in the media was that he could not win without Bill Parcells. Some would say that his legend was built on the back of Lawrence Taylor.

Belichick had always hated the way Parcells had two sets of rules: one for Taylor and the Giants' star athletes, and another set of rules for the rest of the team. For more insight on the subject, read the eye-popping memoir by Lawrence Taylor himself, *LT: Over the Edge*. These impressions were burned into Belichick's mind and would permanently alter his coaching philosophy.

Oddly, as if to prove everybody correct, Belichick immediately went back to the warm confines of Bill Parcells' coaching staff

SPYGATE

after being fired by the Browns. His coaching star had faded considerably.

Belichick was hired by Parcells, who by then was head coach of the New England Patriots. Belichick's role as assistant head coach with the Patriots gained him his first critical contact with Patriots owner Robert Kraft. Parcells had emerged from retirement in 1993 to accept the New England head coaching position.

This 1996 Patriots team played in Super Bowl XXXI, losing to the Green Bay Packers 35-21. After this Super Bowl, Parcells and most of his staff, including Belichick, fled to the Patriots' enemy and division rival, the New York Jets. Amazingly, Parcells didn't even accompany the Patriots players back to Boston on the team plane after the Super Bowl game. This move was a dagger in the Jets-Patriots hate-fest which led to claims of tampering and threatened lawsuits. The Jets even pretended to hire Belichick as head coach with Parcells in an advisory role to circumvent Parcells' restrictive covenants in his Patriots employment contract, barring him from accepting another head coaching position. In the end, NFL Commissioner Tagliabue intervened in this east coast civil war by awarding the Patriots a package of the Jets' draft picks, as compensation for letting Parcells and company out of their Patriots employment contracts.

Once with the Jets, Belichick was again officially named the defensive coordinator and assistant head coach. Things started to click again and the Jets began winning. The Bills (Belichick and Parcells) had the Jets rebounding from a 1 win, 15 loss season in 1996. At the end of the 1999 season, Parcells once again stepped down as head coach, claiming this time he was retiring from coaching for good. He had assured Jets ownership that Belichick would assume head coaching duties, with

Parcells sticking around in an advisory role. However, Belichick had grown weary of the "Big Tuna" and was tired of Parcells' bombastic personality and razor-sharp tongue. There was a particular incident during a Jets game when the two men had disagreed about the use of a blitz. When Belichick was proven to be correct, Parcells reacted most unprofessionally. Instead of being pleased that the play worked out for the team, Parcells barked into an open mike, "Yeah, you're a genius, everybody knows it, a goddamn genius, but that's why you failed as a head coach—that's why you'll never be a head coach…. Some genius." [1] Naturally, Belichick was looking to get out from under Parcells' oppressive regime.

In February 2009 the Jets called a press conference to announce Bill Belichick would be replacing Parcells as their new head coach. What ensued is one of the most awkward press conferences in NFL history. Belichick had accepted the job as head coach in principle the day prior; the press conference announcement was for the media, merely a formality. Before the assembled press and Jets brass, just as Belichick was about to take the podium, he scribbled on a piece of loose paper: "I resign as HC of the NYJ" and handed it to Jets management. [2] He then proceeded to give a long-winded speech about his overnight decision to pass on the "HC" position. This performance could only be described as bizarre by those in attendance. [3] Waxing on about ownership uncertainty and a list of irrelevant notions, Belichick bid farewell to the Jets, as Parcells sat there, slack-jawed. Jets management, fans, and Parcells were blindsided by this bombshell.

Kraft had gotten his revenge. In a move that was decidedly not coincidence, the Patriots fired their head coach Pete Carroll

SPYGATE

just days prior, leaving the spot wide open for Belichick. When asked where he would coach the next season, Belichick calmly responded with, "I haven't really thought about it." [3]

After pondering his future for what seemed like eleven seconds, Belichick accepted the Patriots head coaching position. At this point, the Jets naturally claimed tampering. An NFL team cannot hire away a head coach from another NFL team while that coach is under contract. Since the Jets had elevated Belichick, he was effectively their head coach, if only for one day. In the end, once again, Commissioner Tagliabue agreed that the Patriots should give up a first round draft pick in 2000 in exchange for the right to hire Belichick.

Belichick would bring along Charlie Weis as offensive coordinator, Eric Mangini as defensive backs coach, and Scott Pioli as assistant director of player personnel. Romeo Crennel would follow them in 2001, as New England's defensive coordinator. In light of the Super Bowl wins, and then the Spygate cheating scandal, it is safe to claim there is a lot of bad blood between the New York Jets and New England Patriots. That might even be putting it mildly.

Endnotes

[1] Halberstam, David. *The Education of a Coach*. New York: Hyperion, 2005, 115-16.

[2] McEntegart, Pete. "The 10 Spot." *Sports Illustrated*, July 28, 2006. http://sportsillustrated.cnn.com/vault/article/web/COM1055750/index.htm

[3] Associated Press. "Belichick Quits as Jets Coach." CBS News, February 11, 2009. http://www.cbsnews.com/2100-500609_162-146017.html

Who is Ernie Adams?

Chapter 5

Bill Belichick is often referred to as a coaching genius. Even a casual NFL fan will hear it during Sunday NFL pregame programs. The word "genius" is often tossed around and applied loosely, however. The well-dressed parrot-like ex-jock commentators repeat this trite comment every week. The Patriots' youthful offensive and defensive coordinators have been given nicknames like Boy Wonder or Mangenius. Surprisingly, a great deal of this adulation is undeserved and misplaced by these pundits.

For those who choose to look, it is easy to see that the Patriots have an *Intel Inside*® their secretive football complex. Ernie Adams is stationed up in the coach's box on game day, wearing his thick glasses and dressed like Mr. Rogers. It is Adams, from his crow's nest, who is speaking into Belichick's headset on game day. [1] For years now, this has been the case. When Belichick roams the sidelines dressed in his torn hooded sweatshirt, it is he and Adams who control the Patriots' game plan, play by play.

SPYGATE

He is quite literally a ghost in the machine. Acclaimed for game planning, in-game adjustments, and calling the right audible at the right time, this Machiavelli of staggering influence who controls the Patriots is named Ernie Adams. And no one knows he exists.

Ernie Adams is easily one of the most talented football coaches in NFL history. He is Bill Belichick's right-hand man and lifelong friend. He is, by all accounts, a true genius. He landed his first National Football League job in 1975 with the New England Patriots. He got the job by simply memorizing the offensive playbook in two days. [2] This feat should have taken him weeks.

Without Adams, we would likely not have ever heard of Bill Belichick. It was Adams who got Belichick his first real job in the NFL with the Giants in 1979. Adams had gained the favor of head coach Ray Perkins, and heavily influenced the Giants to hire his friend as a special teams coach. For nearly every NFL job Belichick has had since then, Adams has been toiling in the shadows, taking far too little credit for the duo's many great triumphs. It seems that it's the way Adams prefers things to be.

Adams' duties and responsibilities are always a mystery, even to those who play for the team and work closely with him.

Consider the following quotes:

Former Patriots receiver Christian Fauria described Adams' role as "very mysterious." "He's a guy who looks like he should be working for NASA. I never knew what he did, but sometimes I felt like he was pulling all the strings." [1]

A few years ago, during a team meeting, Patriots players put up a slide of Adams. Below his photo was the line: "What does this man do?" Everyone laughed but even the players do not know precisely what Adams does for the Patriots. [3]

"I don't know what his job title is," ex-Patriots linebacker Adalius Thomas said. "I didn't even know his last name was Adams." Matt Light, longtime offensive tackle, stated, "Ernie is a bit of a mystery to all of us. I am not sure what he does, but I'm sure whatever it is, he's good at it." [3]

Asked to describe how Adams contributed to the Patriots' efforts, assistant head coach Dante Scarnecchia said, "Who?" "Ernie Adams," he was told. "Oh....Well, yeah, OK," he said. "I don't know. Ask Bill." [1]

Former vice president of player personnel, Scott Pioli was asked directly what Adams does. "Some of that information is top secret," he said. [1]

According to Michael Holley's book *Patriot Reign*, Adams is virtually in charge on draft day. It is Adams' keen mind that runs through the teams' value charts that he invented, to find the best value left on the board. Patriots linebacker Mike Vrabel said, "The guy is such a walking football encyclopedia, he is like Google." [1] Belichick himself says, "Ernie's a guy that I have the confidence to bounce pretty much anything off of. I think he's got a great football mind and he's been a very valuable resource for our organization and for me personally." [1] This could be the understatement of the century.

Tom Brady once said of Adams: "The man knows more about professional football than anyone I ever met." [1]

What is known about Adams is this: he is Belichick's consigliere and most trusted tactical advisor. His official title with the team is Director of NFL Research; no one seems to know exactly what this vague title means. No other NFL team has a person with this title, and Adams' duties are a closely guarded secret. He is not an offensive coordinator or a defensive coordinator. He works

SPYGATE

100-hour weeks by his own estimation. [4] But what is he doing when he is at work? What exactly does Ernie Adams work on, holed up in his dark office until midnight? Adams never does interviews and is rarely photographed. The few articles written about him have cryptic titles, such as *Adam's role? It's top secret*; *Who is this guy?* and *Mystery Man*. [4, 1, 3]

The New England Patriots are known as a secretive organization, but why is this man's role excessively top-secret?

The team leapt from last place in their division to Super Bowl winners in just one year. While they were winning two more Super Bowls, rumors were circulating that the Patriots had somehow been cheating. [5] They were finally caught doing so red-handed in 2007, while they were using a highly sophisticated covert taping and communications system. The media would call the event "Spygate."

Could it merely be a coincidence that the Patriots' unrivaled success coincides with the hiring of a person of wide reaching influence, whose duties and job title is intentionally vague and secretive?

Chad Brown was a linebacker for the Patriots, and played in the 2007 season. When asked recently if he noticed anything odd during his time in Foxboro, he remarked that a mysterious man on the New England staff, Ernie Adams, did stick out in his mind.

"He plays a very interesting role within that organization," Brown said. "He's not a coach, he doesn't really talk to players, but he talks to Bill after each practice. They walk off the field, and I guess he's able to act as a second mind, a second set of eyes for Bill…. It's an amazing relationship. Certainly there are times during a game on the sideline, you hear Bill ask for Ernie upstairs: 'Ernie, what do you think?' He consults with him.

Their relationship is shrouded in such secrecy. Even as a player on that team, you can't help but go, 'Huh! I wonder what did happen there!'" [6]

Beyond antisocial, it seems very odd that a key consultant of Bill Belichick, who works long hours in Foxboro at the team complex, never talks to the players. Why would Adams be intentionally quarantined from the players?

Let's start at the beginning. Ernie Adams was a very bright and precocious youngster. He was named coach of his intramural football team at Dexter High School in Brookline, while still in eighth grade. This occurred because the actual coach had wearied of hearing Adams complain that the coach was incompetent. [2]

He was always intrigued by the strategy of football, sometimes referred to as the X's and O's of football. He considered it like battle planning, and indeed, he is a naval history buff. By the time Belichick had arrived at Phillips Academy for a postgraduate year, Ernie Adams had been there for three years. Adams had already earned a reputation as an eccentric. He had quirky habits and dressed like someone from the 1940s. Ernie Adams met Belichick when they played on the same football team at Phillips in 1970.

Belichick's father was a football scout for the Naval Academy at that time and had written a book called *Football Scouting Methods.* The book sold very few copies. Teenager Ernie Adams, certified football nerd, had already devoured it cover to cover. When he recognized Belichick's name at a football meeting, he approached Bill and asked if he was related to *the* Steve Belichick, author and football legend. A fast friendship immediately blossomed. The new buddies played side by side on the team, blocking effectively as a tackle/guard combination for their undefeated Phillips Academy team. However, Belichick was only at Phillips for one postgraduate year to raise his grades, to help him get accepted into a good university.

At night, Belichick and Adams were holed up in their dorm rooms, drawing up plays on notepads and discussing their admiration for Vince Lombardi. Adams felt that destiny had smiled on him, to have a family member of such a distinguished football coaching legend land in his lap. Belichick was already adroit at breaking down game film. He had been studying at the foot of his father since he was a small boy.

By all accounts, Adams was an unusual football junkie. He was a scholarship student and the prep school's top Latin scholar. The year before Belichick had arrived, Adams and a friend went to Boston University Field where BU was having an intra-squad game. He and his friend were up in the stands scribbling notes and drawing up plays. Soon an assistant coach noticed and asked what the boys were up to, and why they were taking notes. The boys said they were scouts from Northeastern, not wanting to admit they were high school football nerds or wannabe coaches. The BU coach told them what they were doing was illegal and they needed to leave immediately. This story was told by Adams himself and appears in Halberstam's *The Education of a Coach*. [2] Adams' recount of this particular story to Halberstam is illuminating. Perhaps this original spying incident sparked and intrigued the young Adams. Early on, Adams was already learning quickly that knowing what an opponent is planning to do on game day would prove critical to a successful battle plan.

On one occasion, Steve Belichick, Bill's father, was in town to scout Boston College and took the boys to dinner. Adams' bearing and intellect impressed the elder Belichick. "What do you want to do as a career?" Steve asked. Adams answered that he wanted to be a football coach. "Where do you want to go to college?" Steve continued. "Northwestern," Adams replied. "Why?" Steve asked. Adams justified his choice not based on football, but "because they have the best Latin department in the country." Belichick remarked that Adams may someday be the only football coach in the country who can speak Latin. [2]

Adams did end up going to Northwestern, a major Big 10 football program at that time. Adams was looking to break into the football program there, so he sent a well-written treatise to coach Alex Agase. The essay detailed the importance of a drop back quarterback in the T formation. Agase was so impressed with the teenager's work that he gave him a job as a scout. He served as a scout for Northwestern until his graduation in 1975 with a degree in education.

Adams was the first of the two boys to land a job in professional football with the Patriots. After Adams contacted the Patriots numerous times, offering himself as an unpaid employee, an assistant coach named Hank Bullough finally called Adams. Bullough gave Adams the offensive playbook to see what he could learn. New England's head coach at the time was Chuck Fairbanks. In two days time Adams had the entire playbook down cold. When Bullough told Fairbanks of this astonishing feat, Fairbanks naturally gave Adams the defensive playbook. Two more days went by and he had memorized this second volume; Ernie Adams is said to have a photographic memory. Fairbanks was so impressed with the twenty-one-year-old's football mind, that he gave Adams a job as a scout.

During his time working for Fairbanks, Adams prepared scouting reports for the Patriots. Fairbanks stated they were the most thorough reports he had received in his career. [1] Adams eventually worked for the New York Giants in 1979, when Patriots assistant Ray Perkins was hired to be the head coach of the Giants. Perkins wanted to bring the boy genius along with him. With the Giants, Adams started working with quarterbacks and receivers. It was not long before Perkins started calling Adam's opinions *Gospel*. [3]

Meanwhile, Belichick was moving from job to job in football and struggling to earn a living, so Adams came to his aid. Belichick's first real job in the NFL was as a special teams coach with the Giants. He had previously bounced around the league with a new NFL team each year, not earning enough money to get by.

It was Adams who had convinced Perkins to hire his pal Bill Belichick. They had made it—both boys now worked in professional football, after a lifetime spent dreaming of this opportunity. "Ernie's recommendation opened a big door for Belichick," Ray Perkins later observed. [3]

Their football careers took off from there. Both men had different skills and talent, that much was clear. But Belichick had something more: ego and a sense of self worth, maybe even too much. In stop after stop, the Ernie and Bill show continued. Belichick got the spotlight glory, while Adams remained hidden behind the curtain, working in dark film rooms, breaking down game film, and giving all the critical data to his boyhood friend. They were experimenting and looking for ways to gain an edge. They consulted statistical studies written on a variety of topics, such as *"when to go for it on fourth down"* and *"when punting is not the safe play."* [2]

Adams pioneered many of the film work techniques that are now commonplace. A popular example includes splicing together all the goal line situations so they can be studied as a unit. Ernie Adams' knowledge of football was without equal. Buzz Bessinger, author of the football classic *Friday Night Lights*, was a classmate of Ernie Adams. "I will always be indebted to Ernie for turning me on to Odessa, Texas," Bessinger said. The famous author attended Phillips Andover with Belichick and Adams. Bessinger was aware of Adams' forte: designing a game plan that would exploit the opponent's weaknesses. Adams had a knack for counteracting almost any defense or offense. "Nine times out of ten," Bessinger said, "Ernie sees something nobody else sees." [3]

After six seasons with the New York Giants, Adams left coaching to be a municipal bond trader on Wall Street. He had always possessed a keen interest in financial markets and his analytical mind was perfectly suited to this field, as well. "I had a real interest in investments," Adams said. "I liked it—every day was competitive, and it was a different part of the world. But it became a combination of enjoying it and missing football at the same time, so when I had the chance to go with Bill in 1991 when he was named coach of the Cleveland Browns, I jumped at it." [4]

By this time, Belichick was a highly regarded young defensive coordinator for the Giants. He was named defensive coordinator in 1985 by Bill Parcells, who had replaced Perkins as head coach. Belichick was only thirty-three when Parcells selected him for this prestigious position. His faith in the young coach was rewarded when the Giants won the Super Bowl after the 1986 and 1990 seasons.

After the Super Bowl XXV win against the heavily favored Bills, Belichick was offered the head coaching job at Cleveland. As soon as he secured the job, Belichick called his friend Ernie Adams to get the band back together. Professionally speaking, the two were like Sonny and Cher. "Sonny" Adams made all the tactical decisions, while Belichick's "Cher" faced the media, taking all the bows. Unfortunately for the duo, in Cleveland there were few, if any, bows to take. As explained earlier, the Cleveland Browns experience was a miserable failure. The Adams/Belichick team was at the helm from 1991 through 1995 with a combined record of 36 wins and 44 losses—a stinging rebuke to the boy genius aura that Belichick had brought with him to Cleveland's head coaching job.

Art Modell was the owner of the Browns at that time. This was before he moved the team to Baltimore in the middle of the night. His team, once relocated in Baltimore, would be renamed the Ravens.

In Cleveland, Art Modell was a hands-on owner in the Jerry Jones mold. He spoke with reporters constantly, and had dinner and drinks with players. All of this drove Belichick and Adams crazy. Although Modell was always around the team, not even he could explain or justify the role of Ernie Adams. At one point this mystery was more than Modell could bear. He famously stated, "I'll pay anyone $10,000 if they can tell me what Ernie Adams does." [1]

With the failure in Cleveland, people around the league started saying that Belichick could not win without Parcells. This burned in Belichick's stomach for years afterward. After the Browns fired Belichick, Adams opened his own investment business, only to reappear years later when the Patriots named Belichick as their new head coach in 2000. Perhaps Adams could only operate efficiently when Belichick was calling all the shots. Twice Adams had gone to civilian life, only to reenter coaching when his partner had complete control of an NFL team. For Adams to work for another head coach, someone who would demand to know what he did with all of his time, was apparently untenable.

Three Super Bowl victories later, most hardcore football fans will likely see Ernie Adams' name in this book for the first time.

The people who work with Adams on a daily basis, where he works 100-hour weeks, do not know what he does. How can this be explained? This is football, not the Central Intelligence Agency. What could Adams be doing that is so covert and darkly guarded?

Read on, and that mystery will be revealed.

SPYGATE

Endnotes

[1] Hohler, Bob. "Adams's Role? It's Top Secret." *Boston Globe*, February 3, 2008. http://boston.com/sports/football/patriots/articles/2008/02/03/adamss_role_its_top_secret/

[2] Halberstam, David. *The Education of a Coach*. New York: Hyperion, 2005.

[3] Thompson, Wright. "Who Is This Guy?" ESPN, 2009. http://sports.espn.go.com/espn/eticket/story?page=adams

[4] Warren, Tim. "Mystery Man." *Northwestern Magazine*, Winter 2008. http://www.northwestern.edu/magazine/winter2008/feature/adams.html

[5] Sando, Mike. "What's Legal, What's Illegal in NFL Spy Game." ESPN, September 13, 2007. http://sports.espn.go.com/nfl/columns/story?columnist=sando_mike&id=3017542

[6] Bouchette, Ed. "The Elephant in the Stadium: Spygate's Cloud of Innuendo Still Dogs Patriots." *Pittsburgh Post-Gazette*, February 5, 2012. http://old.post-gazette.com/pg/12036/1208250-66-0.stm

Spygate Demystified

Section III

The Matt Walsh Interviews

Chapter 6

Star witness Matt Walsh, former Patriots videographer during the 2000 to 2002 seasons, had become restless and bold while biding his time, eager to tell his story to the world. He had been waiting to be fully indemnified against potential lawsuits by the NFL and the New England Patriots. And so he began speaking to a few select reporters while awaiting his interview with the NFL league office and Senator Arlen Specter. Note that it took months for the press and Senator Specter to pressure the NFL into actually sitting down with key witness Walsh. One can only assume he was emboldened by the knowledge that the Patriots would not dare sue him now, lest they appear to be trying to silence a witness.

In an interview with Mike Fish of ESPN, originally published February 1, 2008, Fish was wondering why the NFL never contacted Matt Walsh when the story originally broke. "If they're doing a thorough investigation, they didn't contact me," Walsh said. "Maybe they felt they didn't need to." Commissioner Roger

SPYGATE

Goodell had originally stated publicly that the tapes turned over by the Patriots only documented games back to 2006. But by the 2006 season, Walsh had been long gone.[1] If the NFL wanted to properly investigate this matter, why not speak to Walsh right away? It would seem that he had relevant information.

A few months after the Spygate story became front page news, Walsh made it known that he had potentially damaging information about the Patriots and the NFL, and he had the tapes to prove it. Logically, the league should have wanted to hear from someone who is not currently being accused in the case. As a past employee, Walsh would not have the clear conflict of interest that current Patriots employees would be expected to possess. Nobody had broken any "actual laws"; the scandal strictly concerned NFL league rules. But can you imagine the pressure of being interviewed about the alleged wrongdoings of your current employer? The conflict of interest in question dictates that you would likely want to keep your mouth shut, and keep your job.

NFL investigators astonishingly took the word of the Patriots as the whole and complete story, without speaking to former videographer Matt Walsh even one time.

Walsh stated, "Obviously, Mangini knew what was going on, and it had been going on for a while. [The Jets] tried to catch them [Patriots] doing it last year [2006] and weren't able to. So they were just waiting for them to throw the camera up this year on the sideline." Walsh said that when he worked with the Patriots, very few people inside the organization knew of the team's videotaping practices. Those in the know were video director Jimmy Dee and research director Ernie Adams.[1] Adams and Dee are both currently on the Patriots staff, presumably in the same capacity.

Adams, Belichick's lifelong friend and right-hand man, is a central figure to the Spygate plot. Regarding Adams helpfully shedding light on the controversy, Walsh said, "You've got a better chance of him telling you who killed JFK than anything about New England. There are lots of stories there.... [Adams] told me stories of things they used to do in Cleveland [where Adams assisted head coach Bill Belichick with the Browns]." [1]

Like many in the NFL, Walsh came to the league directly out of college, with no experience. He graduated from Spring College in 1998 with a degree in sports management. He had originally worked for the Patriots in an internship during the first semester of his senior year. After graduation, he had not landed a full-time job and was working as a lifeguard when the Patriots called him, seemingly out of the blue. They offered him a job as a video assistant, even though he had no expertise or training in that field. [1]

Walsh was employed by the Patriots from 1996 to 2003 as a video assistant. "[Taping coaches' signals] was something that they continued to have me do throughout the two years I worked in video, under coach Belichick," Walsh told HBO's Andrea Kremer. "If it was of little or no importance, I imagine they wouldn't have continued to do it, and probably not taken the chances of going down onto the field in Pittsburgh, or shooting from other teams' stadiums the way we did." Walsh told Kremer he was coached on how to avoid detection and what phony stories to tell if confronted by stadium security. Walsh specifically named Jimmy Dee, Patriots video coordinator, as one of his bosses who coached him on blending in and not getting caught. [2]

When asked about Belichick's excuses for taping, Walsh said "Coach Belichick's explanation for having misinterpreted the rules—to me—that really didn't sound like taking responsibility for what we had done, especially considering the great lengths that we had gone through to hide what we were doing." Some examples he included:

"The line of reasoning that we would give to other teams for why we need a third camera setup was, 'Well, our coaches want to have a tight shot of the kicker and the holder exchange, just to go over with the guys in meetings. You know, they want a tight shot, you know, of the quarterback, you know, just to go over the quarterback's footwork and mechanics in meetings.'" Walsh made it clear that the number of tapes made for any one game greatly increased under Belichick. "On average, when you're scouting a team, we'd do anywhere from 60 to 70 cut-ups on offense, 40, 50 cut-ups on defense. Special teams, you're making another 10-15 tapes," Walsh told the *New York Times*. [3]

"When Belichick came along, we added even more to the preparation.... We were also coming into the age of digital technology, too. So we were able to attach statistics to the video, on computers." When asked if he thought he was doing anything wrong, Walsh said, "I had always been a big Patriots fan. I was very enthused, just to have the opportunity that I had the job to work for them. I wasn't going to question what they wanted me to do. They became upset if we filmed incorrectly. I didn't want to imagine what the consequences would be if I refused to do something altogether." [2]

The first game Walsh filmed was the first game of Belichick's Patriots head coaching career. It was a preseason game against the Tampa Bay Buccaneers in 2000. "Once I had done it for the first game, and kind of understood a little bit of the process of how it was going, I actually asked one of our quarterbacks if the information that I provided was beneficial in any way,"

Walsh said. "He said, 'Actually, probably about 75% of the time, Tampa Bay ran the defense we thought they were going to run, if not more.'" [3]

Walsh elaborated, "I had spoken with one of our quarterbacks that said he was called into coach Belichick's office shortly before the Tampa Bay game. In the office was Ernie Adams, Charlie Weis, and coach Belichick. They closed the door. Charlie said to him, 'You know, we've got tape of the Buccaneers coaches' defensive signals. What we're going to do is have you learn this, then we're going to have you next to Charlie on the sideline, when he's calling in the play to Drew [Bledsoe, the starting quarterback], over the coach-to-quarterback communication system.'... The quarterback later told me that within two to three seconds of when [Tampa Bay defensive coordinator] Monte Kiffin sent a play call into John Lynch [Tampa Bay Defensive Captain], Drew Bledsoe had it in his helmet.

"We started using Drew Bledsoe in no-huddle situations in the middle of the game, situations that weren't necessarily hurry-up or a two-minute offense. The idea was presented to me that the benefit to that you know the other team's signals, you got all your players on your field, the defense is on the field. They really can't change personnel if the ball can be hiked at any time. It forces the defensive coach to send in the signals early on, when you still have quite a bit of time left on the play clock. It then gives the offense, again, because the coach-to-quarterback communication system isn't shut off until about fifteen seconds. [This provides] more time to decide what play to call that fits best against that defense, and then still to be able to radio that in to our quarterback on the field—and then have him, you know, transmit that to our offensive players."

SPYGATE

"They'd know exactly which play to call.... There are certainly a number of plays to call that would be of greatest benefit to a particular defense. Seeing how the blitz is coming from one particular side, if you know the coverage is going to roll into a certain area, you're aware of vacant areas on the field, and then, you run a play to that area, you stack numbers to that area. You know, it's going to give you a benefit." [2]

During Walsh's interview on HBO, interviewer Kremer asked, "So when [Bill Belichick] talks about the minimal impact of this, what really bothers you about that?"

Walsh replied, "All that I know, is, the success rate that it had for the first game against Tampa Bay, and all I know is that it was something that they continued to have me do...under coach Belichick." [2]

Rod Marinelli was the defensive line coach of Tampa Bay in 2000, and the Bucs beat the Patriots in this regular season opener. The Bucs' defense had throttled New England's offense all day long. After the game, the Patriots' offensive coordinator, Charlie Weis, was overheard congratulating the Bucs' defensive coordinator, Monte Kiffin. "We knew all your calls, and you still stopped us," Weis said. "I can't believe it, amazing." [4]

It is, in fact, amazing that someone could lose a game in which they knew the defense they were about to face on nearly every play. That statement says everything one needs to know about the controversy. Weiss thought it was amazing that they did not win with this inside information. Indeed, they had a huge advantage; they just were not good enough to take advantage of it. Additionally, the Patriots' coaches had very little time to take advantage of the inside information; a problem they would soon solve.

Kremer also asked about Belichick's claim that he misinterpreted NFL rules. "When I was doing it, I understood what we were doing to be wrong," Walsh said. "We went to great lengths to keep from being caught. Just saying that the rules were misinterpreted isn't enough of an apology or a reasoning for what was done.... Coach Belichick's explanation for having misinterpreted the rules—to me—that really didn't sound like taking responsibility for what we had done." [2]

When Kremer asked Walsh whether the fines levied by the NFL were heavy enough, Walsh said this:

"If they (the Patriots) had to do it again, I imagine they'd pay a $750,000 fine for three Super Bowls." [2]

Senator Arlen Specter made a deal with NFL commissioner Roger Goodell that he be given access to Matt Walsh on the same day that Goodell and his team of attorneys conducted his interview set for May 13, 2008. In advance of Walsh's meeting with the commissioner in his New York City office, Walsh's attorney sent eight tapes that Walsh recorded during his employment as a Patriots staff member. The tapes contained coaches' play-calling signals of five opponents in six games between 2000 and 2003.

Matt Walsh Video Tape Cache: [5]

Tape 1: Defensive signals of Miami Dolphins on September 24, 2000. The Patriots lost this game 10-3.

Tapes 2-3: Offensive and Defensive signals of Miami Dolphins on October 7, 2001. The Patriots lost this game 30-10.

Tape 4: Coaches' signals of Buffalo Bills on November 11, 2001. The Patriots won this game 21-11.

SPYGATE

> Tape 5: Coaches' signals of Cleveland Browns on December 9, 2001. The Patriots won this game 27-16.
>
> Tapes 6-7: Coaches' signals vs. Pittsburgh Steelers on January 27, 2002. The AFC Championship game, New England was +9 point underdogs. The Patriots won this game 24-17.
>
> Tape 8: Coaches' signals of San Diego Chargers on September 29, 2002. The Patriots lost this game 20-17.

The surprise tape in his cache was the offensive signals tape. Up until this point in the scandal, only the defensive signals were thought to be involved, but here was the evidence that the system was much more involved. The offensive signals would naturally assist the Patriots' defensive players and coaches.

Specter, the senior Republican on the Senate Judiciary Committee, had been highly critical of the NFL's investigation and specifically commissioner Roger Goodell's handling of it. So it was by mutual agreement that on May 13th, Walsh was to report to NFL offices at 7:30 AM, and then afterward, he was to fly to Washington, D.C. in order to meet with Senator Specter in his office. Both groups were planning a news conference immediately after the interviews had taken place.

After quickly viewing the tapes they had been sent in advance, the NFL had already begun to issue reports akin to "nothing new to see here" to the media. Seeming to jump the gun, the NFL might have at least waited to speak to Walsh so he could explain what he shot on the tapes and why. After all, the league was being watched closely by big-shot Washington senators, and they seemed to be sweating profusely. The nervous energy was palpable.

In the agreement that the NFL and Matt Walsh finally struck, Walsh's legal team was allowed to retain a copy of his documents, though the materials cannot be used for commercial purposes or in a manner that could "reasonably be expected to be disparaging to the NFL." Additionally, neither Walsh nor his attorney could make documents available to a third party without the league's consent. [7] Is this what Goodell meant by saying, "He is free to speak at any time"?

The NFL also slipped in this curious addition: the agreement stated that any money Walsh makes from his involvement in Spygate during the next five years must first go to pay the costs the league might incur in indemnifying him. The league would then give that money to charity. [7]

When May 13th, the big day came, Walsh spent over three hours at NFL headquarters in New York City. At Goodell's news conference, the league played the tapes Walsh provided for the assembled media. The media members in attendance reported that the advancing sophistication in New England's videotaping practices was apparent, and that the video operator had only one job on game day. That job was to tape sideline coaches as they signaled in plays and formations.

On the tape of the 2002 AFC Championship Game against the Pittsburgh Steelers, the tape shows sideline footage of the Pittsburgh coaches sending in signals, followed by a shot of the scoreboard capturing down and distance and game time. This is followed by two separate shots of the ensuing play, one from above the press box, and the other from an end zone camera. [5]

SPYGATE

On a humorous note, the San Diego Chargers' game tape also included several close-ups of San Diego's cheerleaders performing. The media reported this as "scandalous." [8]

Systematic cheating on NFL games somehow did not merit any serious journalistic investigation, but close-ups of cheerleaders were deemed scandalous.

The most important declaration of the NFL was that there were not any tapes of the St. Louis Rams' Super Bowl walk-through. This was a big relief for the NFL's decided position of "nothing new to report." The league's position was predictable; "the fundamental information that Matt provided was consistent with what we disciplined the Patriots for last fall," said Goodell, who then stated no additional punishment was warranted. Asked if he considered the matter closed, Goodell replied, "As I stand before you today, and having met with Matt Walsh and more than fifty other people, I don't know where else I would turn." [8]

The real fireworks were naturally expected after Senator Specter interviewed Walsh. When asked what he was hoping to learn from a face-to-face meeting with Matt Walsh, Specter became animated: "I want to know everything. I would begin chronologically. When did the first taping occur? Who directed it? And who knew about it? Who participated in it, and what use was made of it? And what effect did it have on the game, as best he could tell? Was there ever any disagreement about using it?" Specter continued, "I think there has been a substantial public reaction that there is a lot of smoke. And there needs to be a determination as to whether there has been a fire, and to what extent there has been a fire." [7]

The Senator was frustrated by the stonewalling tactics used by the league and its teams. Attorneys for the Patriots and New

York Jets had instructed their respective team employees not to speak to Specter. "I got three pages of people who refused to talk to me," Senator Specter complained. [5]

After meeting with Goodell, Matt Walsh flew to Washington, D.C. to meet with Senator Specter in his offices. This meeting ran so long that Senator had to cancel his press conference until the next day.

During his interview with Matt Walsh, Specter learned that during Walsh's interview with NFL attorney and Roger Goodell, an attorney representing the Patriots was in the room, and was permitted to ask him questions. Consider a key witness in an alleged investigation testifies before NFL attorneys for the first time. They are determined to "get to the bottom of the matter," and Patriots defense attorney Dan Goldberg is in the room and asking questions. Does this scenario sound like impartial objective investigation is being conducted? Senator Specter thought this fact "strains credulity." [9] No regulatory body would question a witness for the first time with a defense attorney in the room—it is simply illogical to allow a named defendant into the room when questioning a star witness.

It seems as though the league and Patriots were trying to get the story "straight" with Walsh.

The next day at the Senator's press conference, Specter dropped this bombshell:

> "After a lot of consideration, it's my judgment that there ought to be an impartial investigation, an outside investigation, like the [steroids] investigation that baseball had with former Senator George Mitchell." [9]

SPYGATE

Specter did not rule out Congressional hearings to look into the matter, if action was not taken. To prove he was not bluffing, he marched over to the Capital Building and delivered these remarks on the Senate Floor.

Congressional Record May 14, 2008 [10]
NEW ENGLAND PATRIOTS VIDEOTAPING

Mr. Specter–
Mr. President, the Patriots engaged in extensive videotaping of opponents' offensive and defensive signals starting on August 20, 2000, and extending to September 9, 2007, when they were publicly caught videotaping the Jets.

The extent of the taping was not disclosed until the NFL was pressured to do so. Originally, Commissioner Goodell said the taping was limited to late in the 2006 season and early in the 2007 season. In his meeting with me on February 13, 2008, Goodell admitted the taping went back to 2000. Until my meeting with Matt Walsh on May 13, 2008, the only taping we knew about took place from 2000 until 2002 and during the 2006 and 2007 seasons.

That left an obvious gap between 2003 and 2005. In response to my questions, Matt Walsh stated he had season tickets in 2003, 2004 and 2005 and saw Steve Scarnecchia, his successor, videotape games during those seasons including:

The Patriots' September 9, 2002,
game against the Steelers.

The Patriots' November 16, 2003,
game against the Cowboys.

The Patriots' September 25, 2005,
game against the Steelers, which
the Steelers resoundingly won 34-20.

Walsh stated he observed Scarnecchia filming additional Patriots home games, though he could not recall the specific games.

Walsh said he did not tell Goodell about the taping during 2003, 2004 and 2005 because he was not asked.

The NFL confiscated the Jets tape on September 9, 2007; imposed the penalties on September 13, 2007; on September 17, 2007, viewed the tapes for the first time; and then announced they had destroyed those tapes on September 20, 2007. Commissioner Goodell made his judgment on the punishment to be levied before he had viewed the key evidence.

Matt Walsh and other Patriots employees, Steve Scarnecchia, Jimmy Dee, Fernando Neto and possibly Ed Bailey were present to observe most if not all of the St. Louis Rams walk-through practice in advance of the 2002 Super Bowl, including Marshall Faulk's unusual positioning as a punt returner.

David Halberstam's book, "The Education of a Coach," documents the way Belichick spent the week before the

Super Bowl obsessing about where the Rams would line up Faulk.

Walsh was asked and told Assistant Coach, Brian Daboll, about the walk-through. Walsh said Daboll asked him specific questions about the Rams offense and Walsh told Daboll about Faulk's lining up as a kick returner. Walsh also told Daboll about Rams running backs "lining up in the flat." Walsh said Daboll then drew diagrams of the formations Walsh had described. According to media reports, Daboll denied talking to Walsh about Faulk. We do not know what Scarnecchia, Dee, Neto or Bailey did or even if they were interviewed.

The Patriots took elaborate steps to conceal their filming of opponents' signals. Patriots personnel instructed Walsh to use a "cover story" if anyone questioned him about the filming.

For example, if asked why the Patriots had an extra camera filming, he was instructed to say that he was filming "tight shots" of a particular player or players or that he was filming highlights. If asked why he was not filming the play on the field, he was instructed to say that he was filming the down marker.

The red light indicating when his camera was rolling was broken.

During at least one game, the January 27, 2002, AFC Championship game, Walsh was specifically instructed not to wear anything displaying a Patriots logo. Walsh indicated he turned the Patriots sweatshirt he was wearing at the time inside-out. Walsh was also given a generic credential instead of one that identified him as team personnel.

These efforts to conceal the filming demonstrate the Patriots knew they were violating NFL rules.

The filming enabled the Patriots coaching staff to anticipate the defensive plays called by the opposing team. According to Walsh, he first filmed an opponents' signals during the August 20, 2000, preseason game against the Tampa Bay Buccaneers. After Walsh filmed a game, he would provide the tape for Ernie Adams, a coaching assistant for the Patriots, who would match the signals with the plays.

Walsh was told by a former offensive player that a few days before the September 3, 2000, regular season game against Tampa Bay, he—the offensive player—was called into a meeting with Adams, Bill Belichick and Charlie Weis, then the offensive coordinator for the Patriots, during which it was explained how the Patriots would make use of the tapes. The offensive player would memorize the signals and then watch for Tampa Bay's defensive calls during the game. He would then pass the plays along to Weis, who would give instructions to the quarterback on the field. This process enabled the Patriots to go to a "no-huddle" offensive, which would lock in the defense the opposing team had called from the sideline, preventing the defense from making any adjustments.

When Walsh asked whether the tape he had filmed was helpful, the offensive player said it had enabled the team to anticipate 75 percent of the plays being called by the opposing team.

SPYGATE

Among the tapes Walsh turned over to the NFL is one of the AFC Championship game on January 27, 2002, in which the Patriots defeated the Steelers by a score of 24-17. When the Patriots played the Steelers again during their season-opener on September 9, 2002, the Patriots again won, this time by a score of 30-14.

On October 31, 2004, the Steelers beat the Patriots 34-20, forced four turnovers, including two interceptions, and sacked the quarterback four times. In the AFC Championship game on January 23, 2005, the Patriots won 41-27 and intercepted Ben Roethlisberger three times. The Steelers had no sacks that game.

With respect to the 2002 AFC Championship game, it was reported in February of this year that Hines Ward, Steelers wide receiver, said:

> "Oh, they know. They were calling our stuff out. They knew, especially that first championship game here at Heinz Field. They knew a lot of our calls. There's no question some of their players were calling out some of our stuff."

In addition, Eagles cornerback, Sheldon Brown, reportedly said earlier this year that he noticed a difference in New England's play calling in the second quarter of the February 6, 2005, Super Bowl game.

Tampa Bay won the August 20, 2000, preseason game by a score of 31-21. According to the information provided by Matt Walsh, the Patriots used the film to their advantage when they played Tampa Bay in their first regular season game on September 3, 2000. The Patriots narrowed the spread, losing by a score of 21-16. After the game, Charlie Weis, the Patriots' offensive coordinator, was reportedly overheard telling Tampa Bay's defensive coordinator, Monte Kiffin,

"We knew all your calls, and you still stopped us."

The tapes Walsh turned over to the NFL indicate the Patriots filmed the Dolphins during their game on September 24, 2000, a game the Patriots lost by 10-3.

According to Walsh, when the Patriots first began filming opponents, they filmed opponents they would play again during that same season.

The Patriots played the Dolphins again that season on December 24, 2000; they again narrowed the spread, losing by a score of 27-24.

According to Walsh, he filmed the Patriots' game against Buffalo on November 5, 2000, a game the Patriots lost 16-13. When the Patriots played the Bills again that season on December 17, 2000, the Patriots won by a score of 13-10.

During the following season, Walsh filmed the Patriots' game against the Jets on September 23, 2001, a game the Patriots lost by a score of 10-3. When the Patriots played the Jets again that season on December 2, 2001, the Patriots won by a score of 17-16.

The tapes Walsh turned over to the NFL indicate the Patriots filmed the Dolphins during their game on October 7, 2001, a game the Patriots lost by 30-10. When the Patriots played the Dolphins again that season on December 22, 2001, the Patriots won by a score of 20-13.

The Patriots filmed opponents offensive signals in addition to defensive signals. On April 23, 2008, the NFL issued a statement indicating that "Commissioner Goodell determined last September that the Patriots had violated league rules by videotaping opposing coaches' defensive signals during Patriots games throughout Bill Belichick's tenure as head coach." However, the tapes turned over by Matt Walsh contain footage of offensive signals. The tapes turned over to the NFL and the information provided by Walsh proves that the Patriots also routinely filmed opponents' offensive signals.

Why [did] the Patriots videotaped signals during games when they were not scheduled to play that opponent during the balance of the season unless they were able to utilize the videotape during the latter portion of the same game. The NFL has not addressed the question as to whether the Patriots decoded signals during the game for later use in that game.

Mark Schlereth, a former NFL offensive lineman and an ESPN football analyst, is quoted in the New York Times on May 14:

> "Then why are you doing it against teams you aren't going to play again that season?"

Schlereth said that the breadth of information on the tapes mainly, the coaches' signals and the subsequent play would be simple for someone to analyze during a game. There are enough plays in the first quarter, he said, to glean any team's "staples," and a quick review of them could prove immediately helpful. I don't see them wasting time if they weren't using it in that game.

Walsh said that Dan Goldberg, an attorney for the Patriots, was present at his interview and asked questions. With some experience in investigations, I have never heard of a situation where the subject of an investigation or his/her/its representative was permitted to be present during the investigation. It strains credulity that any objective investigator would countenance such a practice. During a hearing or trial, parties will be present with the right of cross-examination and confrontation but certainly not in the investigative stage.

Commissioner Goodell misrepresented the extent of the taping when he said at the Super Bowl press conference on February 1, 2008:

"I believe there were six tapes, and I believe some were from the pre-season in 2007, and the rest were primarily in the late 2006 season. In addition, there were notes that had been collected, that I would imagine many teams have from when they scout a team in advance, that we took, that may have been collected by using an illegal activity, according to our rules. Later, Goodell said of the taping '[We] think it was quite limited. It was not something that was done on a widespread basis.'"

SPYGATE

Commissioner Goodell materially changed his story in his meeting with me on February 13, 2008, when he said there has been taping since 2000.

There has been no plausible explanation as to why Commissioner Goodell imposed the penalty on September 13, 2007, before the NFL examined the tapes on September 17, 2007.

There has been no plausible explanation as to why the NFL destroyed the tapes. Commissioner Goodell sought to explain his reason by saying during his February 1, 2008 press conference that:

> "We didn't want there to be any question about whether this existed. If it shows up again, it would have to be something that came outside of our investigation and what I was told existed."

On April 23, 2008, the NFL issued a statement that the penalties imposed on the Patriots last fall were solely for filming defensive signals. "Commissioner Goodell determined last September that the Patriots had violated league rules by videotaping opposing coaches' defensive signals during Patriots games throughout Bill Belichick's tenure as head coach." The tapes turned over by Matt Walsh also contain footage of offensive signals.

The overwhelming evidence flatly contradicts Commissioner Goodell's assertion that there was little or no effect on the outcome of the game: during his February 1, 2008, press conference, Commissioner Goodell stated "I think it probably had a limited effect, if any effect, on the outcome on any game." Later during the press conference, Goodell stated again "I don't believe it affected the outcome of any games." Commissioner Goodell's effort to minimize the effect of the videotaping is categorically refuted by the persistent use of the sophisticated scheme which required a great deal of effort and produced remarkable results.

In the absence of the notes, which the NFL destroyed, of the Steelers' three regular season games and two postseason games, including the championship game on January 23, 2005, we do not know what effect the videotaping of the earlier games, especially the October 31, 2004, game, had on enabling the Patriots to win the AFC Championship. It is especially critical that key witnesses—coaches, players—be questioned to determine those issues.

Failure to question—or at least publicly disclose the results of—key witnesses to other matters identified herein on what we do not know.

On the totality of the available evidence and the potential unknown evidence, the Commissioner's investigation has been fatally flawed. The lack of candor, the piecemeal disclosures, the changes in position on material matters, the failure to be proactive in seeking out other key witnesses, and responding only when unavoidable when evidence is thrust upon the NFL leads to the judgment that an impartial investigation is mandatory.

There is an unmistakable atmosphere of conflict of interest or potential conflict of interest between what is in the public's interest and what is in the NFL's interest.

SPYGATE

The NFL has good reason to disclose as little as possible in its effort to convince the public that what was done wasn't so bad, had no significant effect on the games and, in any event, has all been cleaned up. Enormous financial interests are involved and the owners have a mutual self-interest in sticking together. Evidence of winning by cheating would have the inevitable effect of undercutting public confidence in the game and reducing, perhaps drastically, attendance and TV revenues.

The public interest is enormous. Sports personalities are role models for all of us, especially youngsters. If the Patriots can cheat, so can the college teams, so can the high school teams, so can the 6th grader taking a math examination. The Congress has granted the NFL a most significant business advantage, an antitrust exemption, highly unusual in the commercial world. That largesse can continue only if the NFL can prove itself worthy. Beyond the issues of role models and antitrust, America has a love affair with sports. Professional football has topped all other sporting events in fan interest. Americans have a right to be guaranteed that their favorite sport is honestly competitive.

In an extraordinary time, baseball took extraordinary action in turning to a man of unimpeachable integrity—Federal Judge Kenesaw Mountain Landis—to act forcefully and decisively to save professional baseball from the Black Sox scandal in 1919.

On this state of the record, an objective, thorough, transparent investigation is necessary. If the NFL does not initiate an inquiry like the investigation conducted by former Senator George Mitchell for baseball, it will be up to Congress to get the facts and take corrective action.

End of Senate Floor remarks

This earth-shattering account of one of the biggest and most elaborate cheating scandals in the history of American team sports was literally ignored by the sports and news media.

SPYGATE

Endnotes

[1] Fish, Mike. "Former Patriots Video Assistant Hints at Team's Spying History." ESPN, February 1, 2008. http://sports.espn.go.com/nfl/news/story?id=3226465

[2] Walsh, Matt. Interview by Andrea Kremer, in "HBO Real Sports with Bryant Gumbel." HBO, May 16, 2008.

[3] ESPN.com News Services. "Walsh Dismisses Pats' Attempts to Minimize Illegal Taping." ESPN, May 15, 2008. http://sports.espn.go.com/nfl/news/story?id=3396731

[4] Zimmerman, Paul. "Smooth Criminals: Patriots Bring Cheating in the NFL into Modern Era." *Sports Illustrated*, September 13, 2007. http://sportsillustrated.cnn.com/2007/writers/dr_z/09/13/cheating/index.html

[5] Fish, Mike. "One Tape Turned Over by Walsh Shows Patriots Also Stole Offensive Signals." ESPN, May 9, 2008. http://sports.espn.go.com/nfl/columns/story?columnist=fish_mike&id=3387401

[6] Associated Press. "Matt Walsh to Meet with Goodell, Specter on Tuesday." USA Today, May 13, 2008. http://www.usatoday.com/sports/football/nfl/2008-05-12-walsh-meetings_N.htm

[7] Fish, Mike. "NFL, Ex-Pats Video Assistant Walsh Finally Agree to Spygate Meeting." ESPN, April 24, 2008. http://sports.espn.go.com/nfl/news/story?id=3363455

[8] Associated Press. "Walsh Meets with Goodell, Specter." YES Network, May 13, 2008. http://web.yesnetwork.com/news/article.jsp?ymd=20080513&content_id=1443062&vkey=1

[9] Gasper, Christopher L. "Specter Calls for Independent Investigation." *Boston Globe*, May 14, 2008. http://www.boston.com/sports/football/patriots/reiss_pieces/2008/05/specter_calls_f.html

[10] U.S. Congress. Senate. Senator Arlen Specter of Pennsylvania speaking on New England Patriots Videotaping. 110th Cong., 2nd sess. *Congressional Record* (May 14, 2008), vol. 154, pt. 79:S4175–S4177.

The Patriot Way – Black Ops

Chapter 7

"Talk to me, so you can see, what's going on." –Marvin Gaye

"The Patriot Way" is a phrase used to describe the "team first" attitude of the New England Patriots. They do not have any big star athletes with bloated contracts; no showboat egotists are tolerated. They are always well below the salary cap with plenty of draft choices on draft day. They typically gain these extra draft choices by trading away successful players who want (or will want) big money contracts. This would be a pure fantasy for any owner or coach, and seemingly impossible everywhere but New England.

But what if "the Patriot Way" was actually a Black Ops system of espionage that greatly assisted the team's performance? A system, if effective, would explain why the Patriots do things that were considered impossible. That is, until the Patriots starting doing them. If there was a systematic advantage built in to a team's play-calling process, a system one could use on game day to help

SPYGATE

win games, then one could perhaps field the league's best defense with older, washed up players. A coach could create a dynasty with no big free agents and even rookie starters. If that system was effective enough, the players would become interchangeable so the team would not need to overpay anyone. If there is a Pro Bowl player on your team, and he wants more money, show him the door. Let someone else pay him. The next guy in line to take his place can play with equal effectiveness if the system is good enough. Concerning the Patriots, it's about the system, not the players.

Taken to the extreme, wide receivers could successfully play corner. Quarterbacks with no NFL experience, or college experience, could win eleven games or even the Super Bowl. This may seem impossible, but not in New England. All of the above actually happened in the last eleven years in New England. New England is the Bermuda Triangle of professional football, where down is up and up is down. At the Patriots' football complex, nothing is as it should be. No one questions why, we just accept it. We suspend our belief system built on forty years of National Football League games played, and say, *"Wow, those Patriots are really something!"*

Fortunately, we do not have to speculate how the Patriots can do all of this. The Patriots were actually caught using a Black Ops system during the infamous game with the Jets in 2007, outed by a former Patriots coach. They were caught using a system that allows this Bermuda Triangle of football to exist in the great Northeast. However, many fans and media members are not yet convinced that the system amounted to its hype. They wonder how exactly, if at all, this system altered the outcome of the games.

In order to study this thesis, let's start with the basic assumption that for a system like Spygate to function effectively, a team would have to be highly motivated and committed to using that system. This was not casually done. Let us also discuss what a hypothetical football team using a Spygate system would need to have in place, in order to pull off something so complicated—and clearly contradictory to the rules of fair play.

1. A method of gathering offensive and defensive signals; both video and audio communications if possible.

2. A person whose job it is to decode the stolen signs, and a delivery system to get the matching counter plays called in to the offensive or defensive players.

3. Offensive and defensive coordinators the team can trust. The coordinators must be in on the secret. They need to have their designed plays instantly overridden when the stolen signals call for it. Naturally, once you know what your opponent is about to do, you must then call a play that has the greatest chance of success against that play or formation.

Now let us examine the known facts in evidence to piece together what exactly was going on in New England. Let's look at each point that a team would need to see if the Patriots have these bases covered. Based on available evidence, the following was likely taking place:

We already know, from Bill Belichick's own admissions and the testimony of employees, that the Patriots secured video recordings of opposing offensive and defensive players, as well as coaches' signals for every year, starting from Belichick's first game as head coach. We know that these gathered signals were given to Ernie Adams. Ernie Adams, the football savant, can instantly spout off counter play after counter set when given an opponent's play. [1] Adams is hidden from view, like the Wizard of Oz, pulling all the levers that run this amazing machine. It is Adams who enables this shockingly brazen system to tick like a Swiss watch. It is Adams who calls the offensive and defensive plays based on the information he has acquired from the signals others have gathered.

Remember Art Modell and others wondering, "What does this man do?" "Why is he so mysterious?" and "Why is he so important?" Naturally, Adams' job of game planning involves plenty of work that is within the rules. However, someone playing strictly by the rules should not need to hide. In Wright Thompson's thorough article for ESPN, "Who is This Guy?" the reporter wrote: "One former Patriots insider said a videotape of signals wouldn't help the other 31 teams nearly as much [as the Patriots] because they wouldn't have Ernie Adams there to quickly analyze and process the information." Thompson continued, "And if any of this happens to be true [in reference to the Patriots cheating], Adams' love of military history suggests he might see deciphering signals as just part of winning a battle." [1]

Also from Chapter 1, in the interview with Armen Keteyian, Bill Belichick admitted that Ernie Adams looked at the tapes and "if there was anything there he could use, he would use them." Logically and realistically, the only way for a research assistant to "use" the tapes is to call plays. [2] There is no other purpose in acquiring stolen defensive or offensive signals.

It is certain that the Patriots had the signals and a genius decoder. The issue remained of how Adams could get the counter play called in to the quarterback or defensive captain in a very short time window. This significant problem took brains, a healthy dose of hubris, and a serious commitment to cheating.

When the story originally erupted at the Jets game, Chris Mortensen of ESPN reported that the NFL had caught the Patriots using an alternate radio frequency in violation of NFL rules. [3]

Every NFL quarterback's helmet has a one-way radio with an ear speaker so the offensive coordinator can speak directly into the quarterback's helmet. The offensive coordinator tells the quarterback the play that he wants the offense to run. An NFL quarterback's helmet will normally have a green dot sticker on the back of it. This green dot signifies that the helmet is wired for sound; they communicate on only one frequency. What most fans don't know is that this broadcasting of information from the team to the quarterback is automatically cut off with fifteen seconds left on the play clock, by NFL rule. That leaves the quarterback alone with his thoughts to figure out what he is seeing from the defense. He then quickly must decide whether he should run the play just called in to his helmet, or call a different play that might have a better chance of success. If a different play is chosen, this new play is shouted out to his teammates using code words and is normally referred to as an audible.

We have learned from Belichick that the Patriots started using stolen defensive signs from the first game of the Ernie Adams/Bill Belichick era, at the Tampa Bay Bucs game in 2000. We also know the Patriots lost this game, much to Charlie Wies' surprise. At first, you might be tempted to guess the Patriots must not have been a very good team if they failed to take advantage of their knowledge of the defenses they were about to face on almost every play. The difficult limitation that New England coaches Weis, Adams, and Belichick no doubt encountered was the small window of time in which to react, once the defense was revealed.

To explain: the defensive coach signals the defensive alignment in to the captain about the same time that New England's offense is in the huddle. The Patriots' decoder (Adams) had to figure out which defense was called, and then choose a play that would work well against that defense. Adams would then relay that play from the booth to the offensive coordinator on the sidelines, who would then call that play in to Tom Brady's helmet. Brady would then tell his teammates in the huddle, and somehow all of this had to be done in less than twenty seconds.

The total play clock is forty seconds from the end of the previous play. Remember, the quarterback's helmet speaker goes silent at fifteen seconds to snap. There needs to be a little time to get the players together in the huddle, and with substitutions running in and out, this window is extremely tight.

One way to gain more time was to opt for a no-huddle set, which Matt Walsh stated the Patriots would do.[4] This non-action would eliminate the pretense of calling a play in the huddle, and it would have your players set and ready for the audible. However, a team running no huddle for the whole game would probably look very suspicious.

The Patriots finished in last place in their division for the 2000 season; all the while they were using opponents' stolen defensive signs. We can speculate that their system was still in need of tweaking, and they really did not have enough time to utilize the information they had gathered. In addition, this 2000 team probably was not a very good team. Information this critical certainly should have been of some value. And yet they finished last in their division that season. In 2001 that same team, with a few new players, won the Super Bowl. What changed?

After achieving modest returns using the Spygate system, the New England coaches were nevertheless undeterred and desperate to win. Keep in mind this was Belichick's last chance at being a head coach in the National Football League, which fueled his personal incentive to succeed. Failure at this juncture would have been a death knell to his head coaching career. He had already failed in a big way in Cleveland. Two head coaching opportunities, two failures, and a coach is finished as a head coach in the NFL. There are hundreds of millions of dollars at stake for owners, players, and coaches. The pressure to win is enormous. This pressure would be especially acute for a one-time loser, like the team of Belichick and Adams. Remember they are a team. Belichick had the shadow of Parcells over him for many years. People had often said Belichick was not head coaching material, that he needed Parcells to be successful—Parcells himself nearly said as much. [5] But with this opportunity, Belichick was not going down without a fight, even if that fight was dirty.

At some point during the 2001 season, the Patriots solved the issue of "not enough time" by adding a second radio broadcast on a different frequency. That way they could keep speaking to the quarterback's helmet after the traditional fifteen-second cutoff. With the proper technology, it would be very simple to achieve and nearly impossible for the NFL to detect. Anyone can broadcast on thousands of frequencies on any number of commonly available devices. Consider a baby monitor and you get the picture. A one-way communications system is all that the team needed. This second radio frequency would then allow the coaches to continue to speak with Tom Brady after the fifteen second cutoff, right up until the snap, problem solved. In theory they could also speak to Brady while the play was developing, and warn him of blitzes coming from the blind side. Brady is rarely sacked.

The effectiveness of the system would be increased exponentially. The Patriots had no worries of being caught; the NFL would only monitor the official NFL frequency that was in use. Additionally, it was impossible for the NFL to listen in on any other communications coming in to Tom Brady's helmet, due to the one-way nature of the communications setup. This means that the system talks; it does not listen. Quarterbacks do not speak to the coaches.

When Roger Goodell was making proposals in the wake of this scandal, he proposed that NFL security should be able to spot check coaching boxes and in-game communication systems and headsets. It was this secret second frequency Goodell was looking to eradicate. [6]

The following story has been circulating for years. Famed college and Canadian quarterback Doug Flutie was a backup quarterback for the New England Patriots during the 2005 season. Doug Flutie reportedly told John Saunders, a Canadian/American ESPN television analyst, that during one of his first games in New England, he accidentally picked up the wrong helmet with the green dot on the back (Tom Brady's backup helmet) and held it to his ear, so he could follow the play calling. This is something backup quarterbacks do often during a game. Flutie told Saunders that he was amazed that the coaches kept right on speaking to Brady past the fifteen-second cutoff, right up until the snap. In addition, the voice in Tom Brady's helmet was explaining the exact defense he was about to face. This story was revealed by Dan Le Batard, an ESPN contributor, on his talk radio show on The Ticket in Miami, Florida. Le Batard added, "We've tried to talk to Flutie on our radio show about it, but he hangs up on my producer." ⁷ This story has been circulating for years and Doug Flutie has yet to deny the story. He could simply take an interview and take back his words, but he allows the anecdote to remain unrefuted.

It was this extra radio frequency that made the Spygate system so effective. The extra radio communications system even traveled with the team on the road to away games. We know this because it was discovered in use at the Jets vs. Patriots game, when the Spygate scandal story originally broke in 2007. ³ This important storyline was buried by the media faster than the Navy Seals buried Osama bin Laden. Why the media assisted the NFL and its owners in this cover-up is anyone's guess.

When NFL fans and Patriots followers discover how much time, effort, personnel, and technology the New England Patriots devoted to their Spygate cheating apparatus, they will begin to finally appreciate the gravity of what the Patriots actually did on game day, every game. Additionally, this organized skullduggery was designed to be shamelessly contrary to the rules of fair play. This was not an "everybody does it" kind of action. The Patriots entered their Spygate endeavor with a "whatever it takes to win" mindset—essentially the opposite of sportsmanship.

With the new improvement providing additional time to their system, the Patriots possessed an unparalleled weapon on the battle/playing field. The results simply speak for themselves. The Patriots immediately improved, even with a veritable rookie at quarterback.

In his book about the genius of Belichick, famed author David Halberstam made an astute and prophetic observation. The

SPYGATE

author wrote that it was astonishing how a very young "Brady would be able to tell his coach what every receiver was doing on each play, what the defensive backs were doing.... It was as if there were a camera secreted away in his brain."[5] Halberstam unknowingly nailed exactly what was happening, except that the camera was not in Brady's brain, but "secreted away" on the sidelines. Those tapes were decoded by Ernie Adams, and all that near-perfect knowledge was fed back directly into Tom Brady's helmet. All of a sudden, anything seems possible. Rookies are all-pro, up is down, and down is up.

Imagine the confidence and calm a young quarterback would feel, knowing where the open receiver should be on each pass play. It is hardly any wonder that New England had no running game to speak of, by other teams' standards. New England's offense typically moves the ball on offense with a series of short and long passes. Their passing offense is specifically designed to hit the open receiver, which is also why Brady spreads the ball around so much.

But isn't every passing offense designed to hit the open receiver? In many NFL games, one will observe the quarterback going back to his favorite target over and over again. This tight end or wide receiver will have developed a bond with the quarterback and can be trusted to make an important catch in crunch time with the game on the line. For example, Lions' quarterback Matthew Stafford will throw into triple coverage, just to feed the ball to wide receiver Calvin Johnson. Quarterbacks naturally have their favorite targets. Except for Brady, who throws to the open man—but how does he always seem to know who is open?

In his first year as an NFL starter, Tom Brady completed 64% of his passes and threw a miniscule twelve interceptions. His interception rate was microscopic for a new young quarterback. Twelve interceptions for the 2001 season tied him for fifth place in the NFL that year. Only four quarterbacks in the entire NFL (32 teams) had a better interception rate than a twenty-four-year-old kid (Brady), a sixth round draft pick who came off the bench in relief of an injured starter. In his first year as a starter, football legend Peyton Manning completed 57% of his passes with 28 interceptions. Most rookie quarterbacks cannot read NFL defenses very well and have a difficult time adjusting to the increased speed of defenders. Throw the ball too late, it is intercepted. New NFL quarterbacks have noted that in college football everyone is open, but in the pros nobody is open. Brady's performance in 2001 is nothing short of astounding.

Stolen audible signals assisted the defensive players. These phrases could have been easily collected by attaching microphones to defensive players, as teams have accused the Patriots of doing, and then matching the audibles to the plays. [8]

Case in point:

Former Patriots linebacker Ted Johnson spoke to USA Today in 2005, two years before the scandal erupted. According to Johnson, about an hour before game time, a sheet of paper with a list of the opposing team's quarterback audibles would miraculously show up in his locker, and he never knew where they came from—perhaps Ernie Adams? Johnson repeated this story on ESPN SportsCenter in 2008. [9]

In addition, offensive signals of opponents were collected and turned over in the tape stash that Matt Walsh's attorney handed to the NFL and Senator Arlen Specter. A defensive captain would gain a significant advantage if he knew which play the quarterback's audible was indicating.

SPYGATE

Indianapolis Colts' quarterback Peyton Manning, the Luciano Pavarotti of audibles, would be a sitting duck. Every single offensive play, Peyton came to the line to bark out his plans. Unbeknownst to him, he was telling the Patriots' defense exactly what play he was about to run. How did Peyton Manning fare when playing against the Patriots? From the 2001 to 2006 seasons Manning's Colts met the Patriots in nine contests. Manning won three games and lost six games. These games were amongst the worst in his career. In those nine games Manning threw fifteen touchdowns and thirteen interceptions. Three of these games were playoff games, and only once did the Colts advance past the Patriots. In the 2006 AFC Championship game Manning had one touchdown and one interception, but managed to win despite such uncharacteristic numbers. Not coincidently, Peyton's only Super Bowl victory against the Chicago Bears would follow.

On January 16, 2004 Peyton Manning took the highest scoring offense in football to Foxboro for a divisional playoff game, only to be completely throttled by the Patriots defense. The Colts lost this game by a stunning 20-3 score, in which Peyton could not find a receiver open. He had zero touchdowns and one interception. Notable is that in this game, Patriots wide receiver Troy Brown played some snaps at cornerback due to injuries on their defense. He played very well, naturally.

Peyton Manning for his part, did not believe his poor play in games against the Patriots was a coincidence and stopped talking strategy inside the visitor's locker room at Gillette Stadium for fear of being overhead by planted listening devices. Read this post from none other than legendary *Sports Illustrated* reporter Peter King:

I've always heard, reliably, that the Colts never trusted that they were totally alone in the Colts' locker room in Foxboro, and that when Manning had something of strategic significance to say to offensive coordinator Tom Moore, they both stepped outside into the concourse outside the locker room. So if you're outside the locker room Sunday, don't be surprised to see Manning and his first-year coordinator, Christensen, huddling for a few minutes. [10]

Several things about this story should cause any true NFL fan to be very concerned. First, Peter King was born in Massachusetts and is one of the more obvious writer/fans of his hometown team. King would be the last media member to spread unsubstantiated rumors about his beloved Patriots. Next, America's favorite pitchman quarterback feels it necessary to go all the way out in the hallway to speak, so that his words are not overheard by bugging devices at Gillette Stadium. If you have ever been in an NFL locker room, this is a long walk. Lastly, the date of this report is November 19, 2010—three full years after the Patriots "stopped" cheating. Question—how many Super Bowl rings might Peyton Manning own, if the Patriots had been competing honestly?

There is clearly a lot of evidence to support the espionage claims against the New England Patriots. And it is believed by many, including Peyton Manning, that the Patriots did not cease and desist.

The sophisticated espionage system that the Patriots had developed was not limited to defensive signals, and was used to great effect on both sides of the ball. The team's performance speaks for itself.

SPYGATE

Coaches They Can Trust

An offensive coordinator is generally in charge of managing offensive players and all of the offensive assistant coaches. He designs the offense's identity based on the skill level of current players, and grooms new players to fit that identity. Most importantly, he breaks down each week's opponent, looking for weaknesses to exploit. He designs each week's game plan, choosing plays that will be run on game day based on the knowledge gained during game planning sessions. This must be done every single week. He calls the offensive plays on game day, making the critical decisions about play mix, aggressiveness, or when to play it safe. All of the offensive assistant coaches report to him: offensive line coach, quarterbacks coach, receivers coach, tight ends coach, and the rest. Without a good offense, naturally a team will not score many points. The coordinator positions, offense and defense, are the most important positions on the team, next to the head coach. Most head coaches have a background on one side of the ball or the other. Bill Belichick has always been known as a defensive genius. So naturally, he would be looking for the best possible candidate for the Patriots' offensive coordinator position. With his own specialty as defense, Belichick could oversee a great deal of the game planning on that side of the ball.

A multiple Super Bowl winner and perennial playoff team like the New England Patriots could and should have the best and brightest at these key positions. The NFL salary cap, which limits what a team can spend on player salaries, does not apply to coaches. A motivated owner can pay great coaches any amount of money he wishes. Given their results, the New England Patriots are generally assumed to have an excellent coaching staff. They are sitting pretty on three Super Bowl wins, multiple divisional championships, and offensive records galore.

Considering these expectations for coaches, the New England Patriots have made some relatively curious hiring decisions. When offensive coordinator Charlie Weis left the team after New England's third Super Bowl winning season of 2004, the Patriots had an important opening to fill. Going into the 2005 season, the Patriots had a high-powered offense with the best big game quarterback the NFL had seen in decades. Team management had unlimited resources to spend on a new stud coach to fill this important opening. There were plenty of coaches around college and the NFL ranks that would fit well with Tom Brady's style of play.

The lure of the recently won Super Bowl rings and a big salary would create a mile-long list of potential new coaches. So naturally, the Patriots' brass did dozens of interviews with top-notch coaches from college and professional ranks. One would assume they would be looking for that perfect fit of character and experience. In reality, the Patriots made a curious choice regarding their offensive coordinator for the 2005 season.

The Patriots, a perennial Super Bowl contender, oddly chose to hire no one to fill one of the most important roles on an NFL team. No matter; the team did not skip a beat and went to the playoffs with a 10-6 record.

As discussed earlier, much of the game planning and play calling is done by Ernie Adams. While the offensive coordinator was still responsible for calling the plays in to a quarterback's helmet in the New England system, they are not critical to the success of the team. If Adams' role is so prominent, why hide his involvement? Why deceive the public by giving credit to the offensive coordinator and not to Adams?

SPYGATE

Most NFL teams have coordinators with grey hair, or no hair. They have coaches that have been coaching winning football on their side of the ball, and specializing in either offense or defense, for decades. Occasionally, during a rebuilding year, a younger coach will get a chance at a coordinator slot, but never on a perennial playoff contender. The reason is clear: teams simply have too much to lose. If a head coach hires a little-known youngster as a coordinator, and that rookie fails, the head coach would look incompetent. Playoff caliber teams never handle the act of hiring coordinators the way the Patriots handled their hiring. The Patriots might as well hang up a sign reading "no outsiders allowed" at their complex.

There are well over 9,000 football coaches in the United States, many of whom would work for very little compensation. So why did the Patriots hire nobody? The reason is simple: because the Patriots do not need coaches, they need co-conspirators. The New England Patriots coordinators must be let in on the secret Spygate system. On other NFL teams, an offensive coordinator will work through a list of plays he and the head coach have chosen during the week, as part of their game planning process. Those plays are chosen based on the defensive tendencies and exceptional players an opponent may have.

If a coordinator was about to call in a play and Ernie Adams' voice came into his headset, saying something like, "You are about to see a safety blitz," an offensive coordinator who is out of the loop might say, "How do you know that?" Judging by the résumés of the people hired by the New England Patriots, the often highly influential position of coordinator is not given the same level of importance that other NFL teams affix to coordinators. All of the Patriots coordinators, regardless of young age or meager background, perform equally, suspiciously well. They are among the best in the NFL every season, provided they stay in New England. The situation begs the question of why the coaches are the best in all of football while working in New England, but fail to perform when they leave. This is because the actual architect of the New England Patriots offense, and possibly the defense, is Ernie Adams and he is not going anywhere. When the Patriots hire coordinators, no experience or proven ability to mold winning players is required.

Follow this timeline: prior to the 2004 season, the Patriots moved Josh McDaniels (then age twenty-nine) from defensive backs assistant coach to quarterbacks coach. He was a mere assistant defensive position coach. One season later, he was the greatest offensive coordinator in the NFL—an unthinkable progression in coaching skills development. Nearly the same age as Brady, McDaniels had never played quarterback at any level, which certainly denied him background necessary to coach the NFL's best quarterback. So why would the Patriots name their assistant defensive backs coach to be their new quarterbacks coach? McDaniels had been elevated to the quarterbacks coach slot to fill Charlie Weis' void and was asked to call the offensive plays into Brady's helmet during the 2005 season. Only in New England can an extremely young and inexperienced defensive backs coach call the offensive plays. Except he wasn't actually calling the plays, Ernie Adams was.

The 2005 season was the year the Patriots named no one as offensive coordinator following Charlie Weis' departure. Since Josh was new to offensive football, it was unlikely that he was actually calling the offensive plays. As Belichick is known as a defensive guru, the plays were most likely called by Ernie Adams, from up

SPYGATE

in the booth with the curtains drawn. This explains the fact that no matter who the Patriots appoint "offensive coordinator," their offense will run like a well-oiled machine, carving up defenses and moving the ball through a short passing offense, designed to hit the open receiver. It also explains the oddity that any coordinator, while in New England, will suddenly look like the best in the business—and after they leave New England, are below-average coaches at best. Just ask Broncos owner, Pat Bowlen.

At the same time the team was saying goodbye to Charlie Weis as he left to take the head coaching job at Notre Dame, the Patriots also lost defensive coordinator Romeo Crennel. Crennel had accepted the position of head coach of the Cleveland Browns football team. He had earned this shot at head coaching by being a big part of three Super Bowl winning teams. Crennel was replaced by Eric Mangini (then age thirty-four), who was named the defensive coordinator of the Patriots for the 2005 season. Mangini was a Wesleyan University (division III) alumni and fraternity brother of Bill Belichick. Mangini was also a ball boy for the Cleveland Browns when Belichick was their head coach. As mentioned earlier, the two were like brothers. Eric was literally handed the job, no coaching search, nobody interviewed. These men had a secret to keep and they were not interested in bringing new people into their circle of trust.

How did these "best in the NFL" coaches perform in their new positions once they left the friendly confines of Foxboro, Massachusetts? As records show, not very well. As head coach of the Cleveland Browns, Romeo Crennel's record for four seasons was 24 wins, 40 losses.

Charlie Weis' career at Notre Dame started off promisingly but faded quickly. At Notre Dame, Weis was working under a ten-year $40 million contract. After five somewhat underwhelming seasons as head coach, his final record at Notre Dame was 35 wins, 27 losses. At a big time college football program like Notre Dame, that is a dismal record. For his mediocre performance, he was fired, but not before making millions and millions of dollars. It seems that Notre Dame paid for a coach who was not as good as his record of achievement would suggest. Charlie Weis was last seen coaching as the offensive coordinator for the University of Florida Gators. His Gators offense finished the 2011 season ranked #105 in the nation. Doesn't it seem as though Tim Tebow was winning national championships for the Gators about five minutes ago? How does Weis deliver a 105th-ranked offense in NCAA football, from supposedly one of the greatest offensive minds in football—when he was in New England?

Both Charlie Weis and Romeo Crennel had been with Bill Belichick, coaching in his system for years and had long coaching résumés attesting to their capabilities as coordinators, so why the huge drop-off in coaching productivity? We know from Matt Walsh's testimony to the NFL commissioner and Senator Arlen Specter that Weis was brought in at the incipient stages of the development of the Spygate system.

Once Crennel and Weis left the Patriots for much greener pastures, the Patriots could not hire on new blood, like a hot shot coordinator from some other NFL or college team. Because of their systematic cheating, they had a secret to keep. How would a theoretical coaching interview process play out? For instance, during a hypothetical interview with twenty-year NFL offensive coordinator Cam Cameron, at some point Bill Belichick would need to say:

SPYGATE

> *Before we hire you, it's important that you know we have developed a sophisticated spying system that we use here. Often times you will be notified by Ernie Adams the exact defense you are about to see from your opponent. You need to adjust your play calling to this information. In fact, Adams will overrule you on all such occasions. Sound good to you?*

If the coaching candidate replies with the obvious:

> *Well, not really, because cheating is wrong. Besides, if Adams overrules my play calling on all occasions, why do you need me?*

Then Belichick would likely respond with:

> *I understand how you feel, and you're the third person today who has said that. By the way, would you mind keeping this conversation to yourself?*

This is the most likely reason that all of the coaching hires from that point forward have been young coaches from within the Patriots' secretive organization or trusted friends of friends from outside the organization. No prior experience as a winning coach is required or wanted. This would explain why none of these coaches perform as well in their new multimillion dollar roles, once they leave the Patriots. Their new employers reasonably expect that these young coaches have been earning their stripes, as their coordinator titles would normally entail. Years and money have been wasted by the unsuspecting team owners that hire away "coordinators" from the Patriots. Add this to the laundry list of collateral damages done by the Spygate scandal.

Eric Mangini was defensive coordinator for the Patriots for only one year when the Jets made him the youngest head coach in the NFL, at age thirty-five. Mangini did not perform nearly as well as Jets' head coach, as he had coaching for the Patriots. In three seasons at the helm of the Jets, his team had a record of 23 wins and 25 losses. He somehow managed to land a second head coaching position with the Cleveland Browns for the 2009-2010 seasons, where his record plummeted to 10 wins and 22 losses. It was Mangini, of course, who blew the lid off of Spygate when he revealed the system in use at the Jets game in 2007. Being very familiar with the effectiveness of the system, one wonders if Mangini thought much about what the scandal would do to his own reputation as a genuine "great coach." His reputation as "Mangenius" was built on the fact that his defenses were impressive regardless of how many players were lost to injury. Was his nickname deserved? An information gathering system like Spygate inherently made his successes much easier to accomplish. Like all the Patriots coaches, he too reaped the benefits of the system, which boosted his appearance as a top quality coach. Logic would dictate that the Spygate system was a direct contributor to Mangini landing a $10 million head coaching contract with the Jets.

However, if Mangini believed that the system had a very small effect on the outcome of games, only a fool would let the world in on the Patriots' secret. It is clear from his actions that Mangini knew the system was highly effective at giving the Patriots a big advantage on game day. As the Jets head coach, Mangini had lost to these Patriots already and did not want to play on that tilted playing field again. It is worth noting that Mangini has since expressed remorse for having outed the Patriots by bringing the

SPYGATE

Spygate scandal to light.[11] He has said that he never wanted to embarrass Belichick or Kraft by revealing the Spygate system. But one wonders, what did he think was going to happen when this got out, that the Patriots would receive a slap on wrist and everybody keeps playing ball? Ironically, that is essentially exactly what happened.

You may be wondering who took Eric Mangini's place as defensive coordinator when he left the Patriots organization to be the head coach of the Jets. The Patriots named Dean Pees (then age forty-six) as defensive coordinator for the 2006 season. Pees had been with the Patriots for two seasons as linebackers coach. Prior to that, Pees was the head coach of the Kent State Golden Flashes for six seasons. What did Dean Pees do at Kent State to distinguish himself in the eyes of the Patriots front office? For a coach to move from a small-time program like Kent State to the best team in professional football, one would naturally assume Pees was an impressive coach, skilled at game planning and motivating players. In six seasons as head coach at Kent State, Dean Pees' football teams compiled the astounding record of 17 wins and 51 losses, a 25% win ratio.

After compiling a record this awful, how could Pees miraculously run the defense for the New England Patriots merely two seasons later? It seems the only way for Dean Pees' résumé to even get on Belichick's desk at Patriots headquarters was that he was simply a friend of a friend. Pees had coached under Bill Belichick's pal Nick Saban, a multiple National Championship-winning college coach. Saban is a branch of the Belichick coaching tree; he was the defensive coordinator of the Cleveland Browns when Belichick was the Browns head coach.

Pees' first season as defensive coordinator 2006, his Patriots defense finished second in the NFL for points allowed, with 14.8 points per game. He remained in that position for three seasons until the end of 2009. Pees' defenses never finished a season outside of the top eight in points allowed. At the end of the 2009 season, he resigned to take the linebackers coach position at Baltimore; an unusual downward career move, and one not usually made by a highly successful, playoff-caliber defensive coordinator. After Pees' resignation, the Patriots once again named *no one* as the defensive coordinator for the 2010 NFL season. Once again, the Patriots showed that coordinators, whom at every other NFL team complex work seventy hours per week year-round, are not even necessary in New England.

On the offensive side, when offensive coordinator Josh McDaniels accepted an offer to become the new head coach with the Denver Broncos for the 2009 season, he became the youngest head coach in the NFL (then age thirty-two). The title "youngest head coach in the NFL" happened frequently to New England coordinators.

Denver hired McDaniels and gave him a four-year $8 million contract, completing his meteoric rise through the coaching ranks. McDaniels' career from this point on is so illuminating and instructive for purposes of this book that it will be explored in detail in the next chapter.

In 2009, the New England Patriots chose to not replace McDaniels, leaving the offensive coordinator position vacant. The Patriots had just lost the hottest young offensive mind in football in Josh McDaniels. Other NFL team owners were tripping over each other to land the precocious McDaniels. The Patriots, however, yawned and replaced him with an empty chair; perhaps

SPYGATE

they became weary of losing coaches who knew too much about the inner workings of Spygate. Post-Patriots, these coaches kept scoring multimillion-dollar contracts with other teams, and yet were deemed unnecessary at Patriots headquarters. Imagine the late Kansas City Chiefs owner, Lamar Hunt, allowing a charade like this to occur.

It seems possible the Patriots ran out of people, friends of friends, whom they could trust. By not replacing McDaniels, the thirty-year coaching team of Adams and Belichick seemed to be saying:

> *If the NFL thinks the Patriots are great because of these green coaches who were working in college, division III level a few years ago, then we will just win with no coordinators. That will show them who is really doing all the work.*

And that is precisely what they did.

For the 2010 season the New England Patriots employed zero offensive or defensive coordinators! Has this ever happened in the NFL? As if to prove Adams and Belichick's point, the Patriots finished 2010 with a record of 14 wins and 2 losses, earning the top seed in the NFL, all accomplished with no coordinators. These 2010 Patriots also won all of their home games by an average margin of 14 points.

In the playoffs that year, the Patriots suffered a rare home loss to the New York Jets, losing by a score of 28-21. No other team in the NFL had zero named coordinators in 2010; such a thing probably has not happened in the NFL since the merger. Due to the complex nature of modern professional football, concerning game planning and all the work involved, a team with no coordinators is a virtual impossibility. Further, why would any team even attempt to do this?

For the 2011 season, the Patriots elevated quarterbacks coach Bill O'Brien (age forty-one) to offensive coordinator. Let us take a quick look at Bill O'Brien's coaching background.

For his three seasons with the New England Patriots, O'Brien was an offensive assistant, wide receiver coach, and quarterbacks coach—a different role each year. He also never played quarterback at any level; so once again, his appointment to quarterbacks coach was strange. O'Brien was not exactly a specialist at any position. How did he come to be employed by the New England Patriots? Prior to joining the New England staff, Bill O'Brien was the offensive coordinator for the Duke Blue Devils football team. While serving as offensive coordinator of the Duke football team for the 2005 and 2006 seasons, his teams amassed the breathtaking record of 1 win and 22 losses.

After coaching one of the worst teams in college football (possibly history) for two years, how did Bill O'Brien's name ever get mentioned in any discussion of up-and-coming college coaches? Clearly, the Patriots' decision to hire him is totally illogical. How would a coach with this man's résumé even get an interview with Bill Belichick?

And yet, here he was, calling all the offensive shots for New England, who finished as the number #1 seed in the AFC for the 2011 season—all in his first year as offensive coordinator, since his disastrous experience at Duke. Parenthetically, the 2011 Patriots had one of the NFL's worst pass defenses; they strictly made the playoffs on the strength of their offensive prowess.

Bill O'Brien is a local boy from Dorchester, Massachusetts. He played football at Brown University, where he played linebacker and defensive end. He was never, in his football career, an offensive player. He is now being interviewed by several teams looking for a new head coach.

Do you see the pattern here? The coaching carousel in New England is curious to say the least, downright suspicious to be frank. Young coaches certainly get hired in the NFL from time to time. But if a hypothetical Roger Penske is looking for a new driver for his Ferrari team, why not hire Dario Franchitti? You have the money to pay a new man, go get the best. In New England they prefer to hand the keys to new guys with track records of driving cars into walls, and hope for the best. This makes one wonder, why do they do that? A naysayer will state that these other teams might not have had any good players. In the 2000 season, the Patriots placed last in their division, then returned 33 players and 11 starters, who would go on to win the Super Bowl in 2001. The 2001 Patriots did not have many good players either, until a perfected Spygate system was in place. Without that system these coaches do not look as special.

By now, you have no doubt been wondering: *Hey, but didn't they "stop" cheating in 2007? Why does all of this strange hiring continue through the 2007 to 2011 seasons?*

Why indeed?

Steve Young, speaking on the *Dan Patrick Radio Show*, said that the "systematic" nature of the Patriots' taping really bothers him. He said as a player, the effort that went into it (taping system) troubles him. If it didn't make a big difference, why did they try so hard to do it? Young makes a distinction between gamesmanship and what the Patriots did.

"I remember thinking to myself during some of the runs, 'Charlie Weis is a genius,'" Young recalled. "I mean, I remember saying that to people: 'This guy is uncanny, how he's able to make these adjustments and just come out and dominate in the second half.' What it's left me to do is, well, I don't know.... I could see how it could matter if you put it all together."

When Patrick asked Young how big an advantage it would be to know what play the defense was about to run, Young answered,

"The game would be over. If I knew what was coming, that's the whole game." [12]

Endnotes

[1] Thompson, Wright. "Who Is This Guy?" ESPN, 2009. http://sports.espn.go.com/espn/eticket/story?page=adams

[2] Belichick, Bill. "Eye to Eye: Bill Belichick," interview by Armen Keteyian, CBS News, September 20, 2007. http://www.youtube.com/watch?v=Hyg9BhqESxU

[3] Mortensen, Chris. "Sources: Goodell Determines Pats Broke Rules by Taping Jets' Signals." ESPN, September 13, 2007. http://sports.espn.go.com/nfl/news/story?id=3014677

[4] Walsh, Matt. Interview by Andrea Kremer, in "HBO Real Sports with Bryant Gumbel." HBO, May 16, 2008.

[5] Halberstam, David. *The Education of a Coach*. New York: Hyperion, 2005.

[6] Das, Andrew. "I Spy a Problem." *The New York Times*, March 7, 2008. http://fifthdown.blogs.nytimes.com/2008/03/07/i-spy-a-problem/

[7] Le Batard, Dan. "The Dan Le Batard Show." 790 AM *The Ticket*, February 1, 2008.

[8] ESPN.com. "Timeline of Events and Disclosures During Spygate Saga." ESPN, May 12, 2008. http://sports.espn.go.com/nfl/news/story?id=3392047

[9] Christenbury, Jeff. "Ted Johnson: I Received Opposing Teams' Audibles." *Sports of Boston*, February 22, 2008. http://sportsofboston.com/2008/02/22/ted-johnson-i-received-opposing-teams-audibles/

[10] King, Peter. "Giants' Tuck: Stopping Vick 'Almost Impossible', Plus 10 Things to Watch." *Sports Illustrated*, November 19, 2010. http://sportsillustrated.cnn.com/2010/writers/peter_king/11/19/giants-eagles/index.html

[11] Smith, Michael David. "Eric Mangini has 'a lot of regrets' about Spygate." NBC Sports, September 13, 2011. http://profootballtalk.nbcsports.com/2011/09/13/eric-mangini-has-a-lot-of-regrets-about-spygate/

[12] Young, Steve. Interview by Dan Patrick, in "The Dan Patrick Radio Show." May 16, 2008. http://http-trd-l3.cdn.turner.com/si/danpatrick/audio/2008/05/16/DP-Steve_Young%20-5-16_Interview.mp3?eref=fromSI

Say It Ain't So, Josh!

Chapter 8

Josh McDaniels was born April 21, 1976 in Ohio. He is the son of 1997's *USA Today* High School Football Coach of the Year, Thom McDaniels. Josh played wide receiver at Canton McKinley High School and then John Carroll University, a small division III school in Cleveland, Ohio.

McDaniels began his coaching career working under his father's good friend Nick Saban. Josh's first coaching experience was as a graduate assistant at Michigan State University during the 1999 and 2000 seasons. You will recall that Nick Saban is a very successful college coach who coached with Bill Belichick for the Cleveland Browns. By the 2001 football season, McDaniels was a personnel assistant for the New England Patriots. For the 2002 to 2003 seasons he was an assistant defensive backs coach, despite never having played defensive back in his life. Josh was twenty-six at the time he was made an assistant position coach, making him about the same age as most of the players.

SPYGATE

In 2004 Josh made the rare switch from defense to offense, becoming the quarterbacks coach of the New England Patriots. This meant he was, of course, coaching Tom Brady, the most highly decorated quarterback the NFL had seen in decades. Josh was only one year older than Tom Brady at the time, and had never played quarterback at any level. What skills he could possibly have taught a three-time Super Bowl-winning quarterback—one who was rewriting record books—is anybody's guess.

Like so many things in New England, the placement of this highly under-qualified coach stretches the imagination.

As was mentioned in the previous chapter when Charlie Weiss left the team after the 2004 season, the Patriots did not name an offensive coordinator for the 2005 season. According to Judy Battista's *New York Times* article published January 30, 2008, "Coach Follows Dream to Football Summit," McDaniels was the one who called the offensive plays for the 2005 season. [1] In any capacity, Josh McDaniels was a relative newcomer to offensive coaching. How then did this twenty-nine-year-old novice acquire the ability to game plan, break down complicated defensive schemes, choose appropriate plays, and handle all that pressure, having never before done anything remotely like this in his life? Even more puzzling was how he did all of this so well. He was virtually laying waste to seasoned NFL veteran coordinators. Some of these coaches had ten years or more of experience as NFL coordinators. This seemingly stellar performance is most baffling—and suspicious.

When observing these curious hiring decisions in Foxboro, observers are asked to accept as fact that experience is overrated and that almost anyone can be a good coach, regardless of their résumé. It seems like an obvious deduction that game planning and play calling are done by thirty-year coach, strategist, and lifelong friend of Bill Belichick, Ernie Adams. Adams is listed as Football Research Director in the coaching staff roster. Research Director is a position that does not exist on any other NFL team.

Why would the Patriots have Josh McDaniels calling plays and have their resident genius doing "research"? Traditionally, the most important job a coach can have would be to call plays on game day. Why would a professional team give that responsibility to a kid with no major college playing experience, no professional playing experience, no successful college coaching experience, and very little professional football coaching experience? One would never, and it seems clear that the Patriots didn't either. The whole idea of this makes a mockery of the coaching profession.

The next question any observer would ask: Why hide Ernie Adams' involvement? Most likely, the majority of readers have never heard his name before reading it here in this book. You may be tempted to do a Google search, trying to find a picture of him. You will be lucky if you find more than two photos. Nobody in professional sports could be that camera-shy. Adams is like a ghost and the Patriots are going to great lengths to keep it that way. The question is why? What is he doing that is so secretive?

The fact that the 2005 Patriots had no offensive coordinator must have seemed odd to the coaching community. After all, it is the coordinators who become the new head coaches around the league. It seems likely that résumés were sent to Foxboro and coach's agents sought interviews for their clients. Not surprisingly the New England Patriots were just fine without an offensive coordinator that season, finishing with 10 wins and 6 losses. They won a home Wildcard Playoff

SPYGATE

game 28-3 against the Jacksonville Jaguars before losing in the Divisional round to the Denver Broncos 27-13, at Mile High Stadium in Denver.

By the start of the 2006 NFL season, Josh McDaniels was officially named offensive coordinator. No one had seemed to notice that his background would not have supported this prestigious title. By 2007 Josh was already considered a boy genius of offensive football—but of course, 2007 was the year the lid came off of the Spygate taping system.

Having been caught using the Spygate system in the first game of the 2007 season, the Patriots promised they would stop using tape of opponents' defensive signals. It is important to note that the Patriots did not admit to cheating or anything else they were accused of; they admitted only to having "misunderstood" the rules. Then they promised to stop taping signals. They did not promise to stop doing anything else they might have been doing. Remember the NFL had already warned Belichick once to stop taping in 2006 by letter, and he intentionally continued taping as he wished. With Belichick's behavior as a backdrop, only a naïve person would take the Patriots at their word.

The 2007 Patriots then proceeded to rewrite the offensive record books by running up the score on opponents by such wide margins, it appeared they were concerned about their BCS rankings. Does that prove they "stopped" cheating?

To be sure, it was extremely important to the NFL that the Patriots were very successful in 2007. Why is that? The NFL had been saying all along that the Spygate scandal did not mean much because it did not really "affect the outcome of any games." How and why they came to this unjustifiable and illogical assumption has never been explained.

If the Patriots had started losing badly in 2007, all would be lost. The NFL would have been proven as enablers and co-conspirators in the obvious cover-up of the cheating scandal. What better way to prove that the Patriots did not need to cheat than to have the team perform extremely well after they "stopped" cheating. The Patriots also were anxious to prove doubters wrong. Tom Brady was quoted as saying, "We're trying to kill teams, to blow them out if we can." [2] This was after his team was caught and embarrassed. Why he was mad at the rest of the league is not clear, but the Patriots certainly destroyed the league. The 2007 Patriots set records for most points scored in a season, with 589 points, shattering the old record by 33 points. The Patriots would win every game going 16-0 that year. The NFL, and the Patriots, needed the team to play well, or everything they had won would be in question— so they won, and won big.

At the start of the 2008 NFL season Tom Brady was badly injured. Backup quarterback Matt Cassel's success in relief of Brady led many to reach the conclusion that Josh McDaniels was truly an offensive genius of rare and amazing ability. He was offered and accepted the head coaching position with the Denver Broncos, landing a four-year $8 million contract.

The first mistake McDaniels made was trying to bring Matt Cassel along with him to Denver. He could have easily dealt with Patriots insiders to affect this trade. After all, the Patriots had a great trading object in Cassel, and McDaniels knew everyone at the Patriots complex. It would seem that all he needed to do was make the right offer and Cassel would join him in Denver. But for whatever reason, the Patriots would not allow Cassel to go along with McDaniels. The fact that the Denver Broncos already had a stud quarterback in Jay Cutler made McDaniels' botched trade attempt a foolish maneuver. When the attempted trade was made public, Jay Cutler threw a hissy fit and refused to play for his new coach McDaniels. As a team, Denver had plenty of things that needed fixing, but quarterback was not near the top of that list.

It seems possible that Cassel knew the secret to the Patriots' system, and McDaniels wanted to keep that magic going. Or maybe he simply liked Cassel personally; his intentions will likely remain a mystery. What we do know is that Matt Cassel instead went to the Kansas City Chiefs for a song. Also, an irate Jay Cutler shot his way out of Denver, ending up with the giddy Chicago Bears. The best McDaniels could do with the wreckage was accept quarterback Kyle Orton from the Bears as his consolation prize. This was not a good start for young Josh; he was already showing that he was in over his head. His gamble was reckless; to go after Matt Cassel publicly and not get him was a disaster.

It was widely assumed around the league that Matt Cassel would be traded for a first round draft pick to a quarterback-needy team. The Patriots surprised everyone by trading Cassel to the Kansas City Chiefs for a second round pick. Belichick sent this gift to his old pal Scott Pioli, the general manager at Kansas City. Pioli was the director of player personnel at New England for all three Super Bowls. Most pundits were shocked that the compensation to the Patriots—a mere second round pick—was so low. The sports talk radio airwaves were buzzing. Shouldn't McDaniels' Broncos offer have been higher than that? How did the Broncos miss getting Cassel? Why would the Patriots give up any starting young quarterback in the NFL for a second round pick, when a first round pick is the norm? Is there a reason the Patriots would have felt Cassel was not worth a first round pick? Was this a gift to Pioli, or a slight to McDaniels? This event can be added to the laundry list of strange and unexplainable personnel moves that pepper New England's history under Bill Belichick.

We will never know what Belichick was thinking, but of two things, we are certain. Matt Cassel was not nearly as impressive a quarterback outside of Foxboro and the Patriots' system. In his first year in Kansas City as the starting quarterback, his stat line in 10 games of play was as follows:

> Pass completion rate: 55% for 2,924 yards
> Touchdowns: 16   Interceptions: 16

That season followed a full successful season in New England, where his stat line was:

> Pass completion rate: 63% for 3,693 yards
> Touchdowns: 21   Interceptions: 11

It is important to remember this season in New England was Cassel's first season as a starting quarterback since his high school days. His performance in Kansas City is what one would expect from a quarterback of his experience level, making his performance in New England mind-blowing.

The contract Cassel received in Kansas City was six years, $62.7 million, with $28 million guaranteed. These contract figures become even more significant in the next chapter.

Back in Denver things were getting worse for McDaniels. His initial season as the Broncos' head coach began to unravel as he got into a very public feud with All-Pro wide receiver Brandon Marshall. McDaniels was unable to gain control of the petulant star, eventually trading Marshall away to the Miami Dolphins.

SPYGATE

It seemed that the pressure of being a head coach was getting to Josh. However, he brought a friend along with him from his glory days in New England. His Director of Video Operations, Steve Scarnecchia, had joined McDaniels' staff when he first moved west to assemble his team. Scarnecchia had been intimately involved in the original Spygate incident as a video assistant, who was specifically named by Matt Walsh in his testimony to Senator Specter. Walsh was on record, identifying Scarnecchia as the man who actually taped opponents' signals during Patriot games. Why McDaniels would bring a tainted employee along to his new dream job, observers can only imagine. Not surprisingly, soon enough, they were up to their old tricks.

In early November 2010, a six-minute film of a San Francisco 49ers walk-through prior to their game on October 31st was turned over to NFL security by the Denver Broncos' front office. The tape had been shot by Steve Scarnecchia while he was on location for a Broncos versus 49ers game played in London, England.[3] When this tape made its way into the hands of a Broncos front office employee, they immediately alerted Pat Bowlen, the owner of the Denver Broncos. NFL security was notified and they swept into Denver like a SWAT team.[4]

Like old, trusted friends do, Scarnecchia fell on his sword for McDaniels; he claimed he had made the tape on his own, he knew it was wrong, and nobody (McDaniels) had ever told him to do anything like that ever before.[5] It seems that audiences were supposed to believe that the tape was for Steve's considerable private collection of illegal tapes.

McDaniels claimed that he had never looked at the tape himself, not even once—but the damage had been done.

Denver Broncos brass was mortified. [6] They had done the honorable thing and immediately notified NFL security once they became aware of the violation. But the question soon became obvious as to whether they had hired an imposter. The Broncos offense under McDaniels' control was ranked 20th in points scored in his first season of 2009. By the 2010 season, the team was floundering. All the while, the Broncos had considerable talent on that side of the ball. (The 2011 Broncos would make it to the divisional round of the NFL playoffs with a new head coach.) McDaniels was not showing any of the magic he had displayed while coaching the high-scoring Patriots. The Broncos' front office and owner Pat Bowlen were embarrassed and furious.

McDaniel had some explaining to do. So Josh called a meeting with his coaching staff, trying desperately to get back some of his lost credibility. Josh started the meeting by threatening his staff with this warning: "If this gets out, there are jobs on the line," translating to: If you repeat this, you will be fired. He went on to explain that this Spygate II incident (as the media would call it) did not show him as the kind of person he was at all. This was a one-time incident by a rogue employee, who had already been fired.

He continued with this remarkable statement: This is not like in New England, where "that was practiced, that was coached, that was worked on." [5]

Well he ought to know! Josh was at the very center of the Spygate system since its creation in 2001. This is likely why he was made the Patriots "offensive play caller" when nothing on his résumé would have supported such a role. He was a necessary pawn in the apparatus. Josh would clearly be a primary beneficiary of that sophisticated cheating system. Knowing what the defense is trying to do would make offensive play-calling much easier. After all, the system that bought him his "boy wonder" status was located in New England. In Denver without the system, McDaniels had to rely on his true, albeit less than wonderful, abilities.

Since his quotes are printed here, it is safe to say his secret left the room. The coaching staff was not impressed by the unprofessional way Josh threw his old team under the bus while trying to clear his name. His staff immediately reported this event to Jay Glazer of Fox Sports. The other staff members undoubtedly questioned McDaniels' statements, considering his past in New England. Conversations might have gone:

> *Hey, wait a minute Josh, weren't you one of the people in New England working on and perfecting the cheating system with Steve Scarnecchia? Why would you absurdly claim that that is not who you are? Why else would you bring Scarnecchia here, if not to recreate that clever scheme?*

The NFL did a full investigation and found no widespread corruption at the Broncos facility. This investigation included a forensic sweep of computer equipment in the coaches' offices.

The NFL handed down a fine of $50,000 to Josh McDaniels and additionally fined the Broncos $50,000. They concluded that McDaniels did not deserve to be suspended because he never looked at the tape. However, they only took his word on that particular claim.

In handing down his punishment, NFL Executive Vice President Jeff Pash was asked by the media why the punishment for the Broncos was significantly less than the fines imposed on the Patriots for a similar crime. Pash responded:

> *"I think with any disciplinary action, you have to focus on what exactly the facts are. Here you had, as best we can conclude, a single incident as opposed to, in New England, years of activity. You had an incident that, as best we could identify, was carried out by a single employee without direction from the coaching staff or anyone else at the club. That's obviously different from what we saw in New England where the head coach was actively supervising the activity."* ³

An amazing declaration of guilt was laid on Belichick's head by the Executive Vice President of the NFL.

The sacrificial lamb, videographer Steve Scarnecchia, was barred from the NFL for life. Scarnecchia's father also currently works in the NFL; Dante Scarnecchia is actually the current assistant head coach and offensive line coach of the New England Patriots. Ironically, the New England Patriots' current assistant head coach's son, Steve Scarnecchia, is serving a lifetime suspension from the NFL—for being a repeat Spygate offender.

It seems odd that McDaniels was not also treated as a repeat offender. Luckily for Josh, Scarnecchia was the willing scapegoat, and McDaniels once again got away essentially scot-free—except that the highly-embarrassed Broncos now had McDaniels on a very short leash. The Broncos had already started the 2010 season with 3 wins and 9 losses. The losses were ugly and the offense was going nowhere. But the straw that broke the camel's back was the Spygate II incident. Josh McDaniels was fired less than one month after this taping scandal sequel became public.[6] Amazingly, Josh was not fired "for cause"; in doing so, the Broncos were still on the hook for $7 million still owed to McDaniels per his contract.

Looking for a new coaching position, Josh decided to take his talents to St. Louis. The St. Louis Rams had a number one overall pick at quarterback in Sam Bradford. Bradford is a legitimate franchise quarterback, a Heisman Trophy winner from Oklahoma. The Rams also had perhaps the best power running back in the NFL—Steven Jackson. All they needed was a good offensive coordinator, so a deal was struck and Josh moved to St Louis.

For the 2011 football season Josh McDaniels was the offensive coordinator for the St. Louis Rams. Although mentioned by several analysts as a preseason team to watch, helped by the fact that they were competing in a weak NFC west division, the Rams finished the 2011 season with the 31st ranked offense out of 32 teams. The Rams' record for the 2011 season was two wins, fourteen losses.

How did the greatest young offensive mind in the NFL, while in New England, become one of the worst offensive coordinators in the NFL? The reason is simple: he left New England. If Josh McDaniels was even half the coach that he appeared to be while he was coaching the New England Patriots, why weren't his post-Patriots offenses ranked somewhere in the mid-teens range, instead of at the bottom of the NFL ranks? That question is not meant to suggest that he must stay the best coordinator everywhere he coaches. There is a lot of variability in any team's performance and factors beyond Josh's control. But how did he go from "the best young coordinator in history" based on the 2007 season's record-setting standards to one of the worst coordinators in the league? It cannot be due to the players; New England has new players every year, including an all important quarterback switch to Matt Cassel. As a side note, the aforementioned variability in an NFL team's performance is exactly what we do not see in New England. They perform well every year, regardless of players, regardless of coordinators. And now you know why.

Ironically, Josh McDaniels is currently back coaching the Patriots' offense in New England. As this book was being written, Penn State hired 2011 Patriots offensive coordinator Bill O'Brien to be their new head coach. Penn State fans and alumni association the Letterman's Club alertly pointed out that O'Brien has a very thin résumé as a successful coach—a very accurate observation regarding all of the Patriots coordinators over the last ten years. Denver Broncos owner Pat Bowlen probably wishes he had looked a little closer at the résumé of a certain assistant defensive backs coach from John Carroll University named Josh.

With an important coaching opening, naturally the Patriots would turn to an insider, someone they could trust, so they hired Josh McDaniels back. No interviews, no coaching searches. The circle of trust is very tight in Foxboro. The Patriots hired McDaniels, even after he pointed the finger of blame in their direction, with his recent statements regarding the second Spygate incident. After all, he was just telling the truth. Given his unimpressive record, why did New England want McDaniels back? Is Josh McDaniels a good coach? Odds are, he will be in New England.

Endnotes

[1] Battista, Judy. "Coach Follows Dream to Football's Summit." *The New York Times*, January 30, 2008. http://www.nytimes.com/2008/01/30/sports/football/30patriots.html

[2] Brady, Tom. Interview on WEEI Radio. November 21, 2007. http://besteversportstalk.blogspot.com/2007/11/tom-brady-were-trying-to-kill-teams.html

[3] Fallon, Julie. "Broncos Spygate 2: Will the fingers be pointed at Bill Belichick again?" *The Christian Science Monitor*, November 29, 2010. http://www.csmonitor.com/USA/Sports/2010/1129/Broncos-Spygate-2-Will-the-fingers-be-pointed-at-Bill-Belichick-again

[4] Couch, Greg. "Broncos' Spygate Reeks of Cover-Up." AOL News, November 27, 2010. http://www.aolnews.com/2010/11/27/broncos-spygate-reeks-of-cover-up/

[5] Florio, Mike. "Report: McDaniels Explains to Coaching Staff Differences Between Spygate I and II." NBC Sports, November 28, 2010. http://profootballtalk.nbcsports.com/2010/11/28/report-mcdaniels-explains-to-coaching-staff-differences-between-spygate-i-and-ii/

[6] Klis, Mike. "McDaniels Fired as Broncos Coach After Controversy, Losses Pile Up." *The Denver Post*, December 6, 2010. http://www.denverpost.com/broncos/ci_16791509

Why No Love for Brady?

Chapter 9

The National Football League has never been more popular than it is right now. It is a colossal business empire awash in cash. Currently it is a business worth $9 billion a year. Every time the NFL renegotiates its rates for broadcast partners, the price rates increase by massive increments. The newest broadcasting deal signed by the league and its broadcast partners featured a 60% increase over the prior contracts. ESPN alone will pay $1.9 billion just for the right to broadcast Monday Night Football. That is $1.9 billion every season, until the year 2021. $1.9 billion is 73% more than ESPN paid in its last contract. The NFL has become must-see TV. [1]

Every team in the NFL makes money thanks to revenue sharing. Revenue sharing is a gift to the league from legendary Giants owner Wellington Mara. The late Wellington Mara owned the team with the biggest media market in New York City, and could have kept all the big money for himself, the way that major market baseball teams have done in Major League Baseball. It is this massive disparity in local revenue that allows big city baseball teams to wildly outspend smaller market teams when acquiring free agent players.

Mara correctly saw into the future, where a league with many competitive teams would be much better for fan interest, growing the popularity of the league as a whole. As a rising tide lifts all boats, the NFL model is the envy of sports franchises around the globe.

Without this sharing of wealth and a hard salary cap limiting the amount any team can spend on its players, the NFL would not be nearly as much fun for fans. Without these rules, it is unlikely that a little village called Green Bay in Wisconsin could compete head to head with a team from New York City, arguably one of the most important cities on the planet.

The exact economics of NFL ownership is a guarded secret, but with very little trouble we can estimate just how great NFL owners have it. The *Wall Street Journal* reported in December of 2011 that the NFL's new media deals with its broadcast partners alone, call for total cash payment of nearly $6 billion per season. This is just broadcasting—no apparel, no licensing, etc. If only this contract were distributed evenly to the 32 teams, each club would get a check for around $190 million per season. With the 2011 salary capped at $120 million, even an average businessman can make a comfortable living by owning an NFL team. Adding revenue on top of the broadcasting deal is ticket sales, national and local advertising sales, jerseys sales, beer and food at the stadiums…The list of profitable sources of revenue is endless.

This brings us to a major gap in the wealth of NFL owners. That split concerns the ownership of the stadiums in which their teams play. The top five most valuable teams in the NFL all own their home stadiums. As of the *Forbes Magazine* 2011 valuation, in order, they are as follows: [2]

>Dallas Cowboys:
>worth $1.8 billion, owner Jerry Jones
>Washington Redskins:
>worth $1.5 billion, owner Daniel Snyder
>New England Patriots:
>worth $1.4 billion, owner Robert Kraft
>New York Giants:
>worth $1.3 billion, owners John Mara and Steve Tisch
>New York Jets:
>worth $1.2 billion, owner Woody Johnson

As a point of reference, the Jacksonville Jaguars are worth $725 million, ranked #32 at the bottom of the NFL pile. The Jaguars pay rent to play in their home stadium, which is owned by the city of Jacksonville.

Paper magnate Robert Kraft came to own the New England Patriots through an unusual business maneuver in the late 1980s. He first took control of Sullivan stadium where the Patriots were playing at that time. That field is commonly known as Foxboro Stadium for its location in Foxboro, Massachusetts.

In 1985, Kraft bought an option on land adjacent to the stadium as his first chess move. Then in 1988, Kraft would outbid several competing bidders to buy Sullivan stadium out of bankruptcy court from Billy Sullivan for $25 million. This would later prove a masterstroke that would give Kraft much needed leverage to land the real prize, the National Football League Patriots team itself.

SPYGATE

In 1992, St. Louis businessman, James Busch Orthwein bought the team from then owner Victor Kiam, who was facing a bankruptcy proceeding. It soon became clear that Busch, grandson of Adolphus Busch, founder of Anheuser-Busch Beer Company, was intending to move the team to his hometown of St. Louis. St. Louis had recently lost their beloved NFL Cardinals to Arizona in 1988.

Kraft, a lifelong Patriots fan, was not about to let that same fate befall Boston. He refused to allow Orthwein out of the Patriots long-term lease with his Sullivan Stadium, even turning down $75 million cash to settle the matter. Trapped in Boston, a frustrated Orthwein accepted a then-record $175 million counter offer from Robert Kraft for the outright purchase of the Patriots Football franchise. It was a risky move for Kraft on many levels. For one, Kraft had to scrape together the money; $175 million was a lot of money for him at that time in his life. Secondly, the Patriots at that point were not exactly an NFL powerhouse. They never won anything and they were among the least valuable franchises in the NFL. But Kraft had a dream and he risked everything to see it become a reality.

For his dream and substantial risk to pay off, the team needed to be successful. The Patriots already had a great fan base, but to really make big money in the NFL, you have to field a winning product.

After a few years of struggling and some success, notably with Bill Parcells, the Patriots finally landed a long-term answer for the 2000 season when Kraft enticed Bill Belichick away from the Jets. Kraft would be rewarded as Belichick proceeded to completely turn the franchise around in just one season. At the end of the 2001 season they were crowned Super Bowl Champions.

The captain of this starship was Tom Brady, a sixth round draft choice who took the NFL by storm.

But Tom terrific was not done; he topped that by winning two more Super Bowls within four years, a feat never before accomplished and one that should have been nearly impossible in the free agency era.

With true player free agency starting in the early 90s, players could move from team to team more easily, making it difficult to keep a highly successful team together for very long.

The only true constant in New England is Tom Brady and Bill Belichick (and Ernie Adams). Given all of the success that has been attributed to Tom Brady's play, one would assume that he is one of the most valuable quarterbacks in the NFL. His leadership and amazing success have made Robert Kraft's big gamble pay off handsomely. The Patriots have gone from the NFL cellar to the penthouse suite in a few short years. Not just in the trophy case, but in the team coffers as well. Kraft's windfall has come from fielding a championship team in a huge media market like Boston, Massachusetts.

Why then, is Tom Brady known to some as "the greatest quarterback to ever play in the NFL" the most poorly paid superstar in American team sports history? There is not a player in any team sport who has been disrespected the way Brady has by New England Patriots management.

When it comes to compensation Brady has been serially underpaid. NFL fans will recall that in 2010 Brady signed a big extension that made him one of the highest paid players in the NFL. However, let us take a look back to a time before the world knew about Spygate and the cheating system the Patriots had perfected.

SPYGATE

Consider the facts:

Tom Brady was drafted in the year 2000 and won the Super Bowl in 2001. For the 2001 season Brady was paid $314,000. Being that he was a sixth round draft choice, his pay was commensurate with that draft slot. After winning the Super Bowl, the team wanted to reward Brady, so they gave him a new contract that paid him $3.8 million for the 2002 season. That contract figure ranked him as the #22 highest paid quarterback in the NFL. Still, the compensation was completely understandable; Brady got a tenfold pay raise and the team was holding all the cards. He was still playing under his rookie contract, so he could not go anywhere for a while. Not only that, his first year could have been a fluke, a lightning bolt, never to be repeated. All in all, his pay raise was a decent deal for both parties.

However, his performance was not a fluke, the kid had skills! He won two more Super Bowls in quick succession and turned the NFL world on its ear. When Brady won his third Super Bowl in 2004, he had been paid $5.5 million for the season. That pay rate ranked him #14 highest paid quarterback in the NFL that year.

The time had come for Brady to really get paid; and now he held all the cards. He had put his time in, worked through five seasons, and delivered an unheard-of three Lombardi trophies. During the offseason, Brady and his agent made it known they were looking for a new deal. The saying goes that in life, timing is everything, and Brady's timing could not have been better. Both Peyton Manning and Michael Vick had just signed long-term mega-million-dollar contracts. All three players had come into the NFL around the same time. Both Manning and Vick were selling out games and producing highlights every night on ESPN Sports

Center, but neither signal caller had even smelled a Super Bowl trophy, much less won three. By 2005 Manning had a very poor playoff record of three wins and five losses, many times losing in the first playoff game. Vick had been to the playoffs twice, winning two games, and losing two. Neither was anywhere near the lofty level of play to which Tom Brady had ascended.

For the 2004 season Manning and Vick signed contracts that were very similar to one another:

Manning: $99.2 million, 7 years, $34 million guaranteed
Vick: $130 Million, 10 years, $37 million guaranteed

They both signed essentially the same deal: $13-14 million per season, over slightly different time periods.

One would assume that Brady would be worthy of the same, if not more money, to the World Champion New England Patriots. It seemed to all observers that Tom Brady was the glue to everything Patriots. He was a model citizen and never had so much as a traffic ticket. Movie star handsome, Brady is a winner on a scale that is hard to exaggerate. He dates supermodels and actresses, and fans and media alike adore him.

In the offseason before the 2005 season the Patriots had just come off a Super Bowl win; the timing could not have been better for Brady to strike a huge paycheck. Contract negotiations started with Brady richly deserving a raise. However, his bid was knocked down by Patriots owner Robert Kraft, who flat-out refused to pay him. Brady was the most important player to his team in the NFL, and was inexplicably told to lower his expectations. Kraft said that the team was not willing to pay anywhere near the amount of money other quarterbacks were receiving. [3]

SPYGATE

This kind of disrespect is rarely, if ever witnessed in sports. Whenever a critical player in a team sport has delivered multiple championships to his team, and the time comes for a new contract, that player sets the bar as one of the highest paid in the league. Blockbuster contracts in this situation are expected in any league and any sport.

The reason teams always pay their most important superstars is obvious. There are thirty-one other teams that would pay him justly if he was unhappy and wanted to leave. The player does not have to sign a below-market contract and the owner cannot force him to play. Any ensuing media battle or holdout by the player would result in a fan revolt of the French Revolution variety.

For instance, what if Tom Brady's agent told a Boston beat reporter, "Robert Kraft won't pay my client the money he richly deserves." If his agent said, "My guy worked his tail off, delivered three world titles, and Kraft thinks that he doesn't deserve Manning's money. So I am instructing my client to hold out and he won't be at training camp this year." Fans would have been outraged by the team's greedy owner. Robert Kraft might have been burned at the stake in Gillette Stadium by season ticket holders.

But Brady did not say a word to the press; he kept his cool, except to say that he was frustrated by the lack of progress on a new long term contract. This mind-blowing contract impasse went on for months.

Imagine Dallas Cowboys owner Jerry Jones allowing Tom Brady to get "frustrated" over a new contract, given this same set of circumstances. Jones, after admiring his own grinning face in the shiny silver surfaces of his three new Super Bowl trophies, might have offered personal deep tissue massages to Brady, just to get negotiations off on the right foot.

Redskins mercurial owner Dan Snyder might have delivered $40 million worth of gold bullion with his personal helicopter to the front lawn of Tom Brady's beach house, given this same opportunity. Why would any owner let a player as important as Brady get frustrated? Just pay the man!

But not Kraft, he wasn't budging. He was even quoted in the media stating that the team would not pay the kind of guaranteed money just received by Vick and Manning. [3] Tom Brady likely considered this a slap in the face.

The obvious question is why Kraft chose not to pay his savior, as any NFL team owner would have done? Brady had been wiping the floor with Manning at every opportunity, how could he possibly be worth less money? And he had won three Super Bowl titles to Manning's zero. Tom Brady should have had all the leverage in these negotiations, and the Patriots should have had very little, if any at all.

If that seems unfair, consider the fact that for Vick and Manning, this was not their first, but their second big contract.

Vick and Manning were drafted number one overall in their respective drafts. Manning had already collected every penny of a $48 million rookie contract. Vick had worked through four years of a six-year $62 million deal. Each player had already banked nearly $50 million and delivered five playoff wins combined.

Whatever the reason for Kraft undervaluing Brady, we know that Brady eventually agreed with this massive undervaluation. After all, he signed the contract. Tom Brady and his agent agreed to this relatively meager agreement.

Brady's 2005 contract turned out to be $60 million, 6 years, $26 million guaranteed—approximately the same as Eli Manning's rookie contract signed in 2004.

SPYGATE

For a man of his apparent abilities and trophy case of accomplishments, this contract is hard to fathom. Essentially, 40% less than his "peer group," if one considers Manning and Vick his peers. Brady should have been paid much more money based on his play, and he easily could have made that happen. The question is why did this exploitation of Brady occur, but more importantly, why did he stand down and allow it to happen?

In the aptly named article "Another Patriot Victory," published May 9, 2005, Peter King of *Sports Illustrated* wrote:

> Peyton Manning's making $14.2 million a year, with the Colts, and he signed that deal a year ago, Brady could have said: *You guys are high if you think I'm doing a deal for $10 million a year—especially after ESPN just raised the ante ridiculously with the new broadcast contract.* [4]

King continued by praising the wise quarterback for taking this seemingly inequitable deal because Brady "gets it." King's idea of wisdom is to leave money on the table for others because there is only so much money under the salary cap each year. More money for other players means the Patriots will have a better team. He quotes Brady directly as stating: "Is it going to make me feel any better to make an extra million, which, after taxes, is about $500,000? That million might be more important to the team." [4]

The gap in logic here is startling. Firstly, two paragraphs later King accurately points out that the difference in Manning's contract and Brady's new contract was $4 million *per season*, not "an extra million." Also, the Patriots are nearly always well below the salary cap and don't pay big money to free agents. What King fails to realize is that this contract was completely unfair to Brady.

He was being paid like a great NFL linebacker, not a once in a lifetime quarterback.

Clearly, a contract this slanted in the Patriots' favor could have been negotiated in about one hour. But this contract took months of "frustrated" negotiations between the team, Brady and his agent.

While the majority of readers will laugh at anyone calling a $60 million contract "exploitation," bear in mind that Brady left at least $30 million on the table. Why leave more money in a billionaire owner's pocket? This $30 million-plus he left on the table amounted to a gift to Robert Kraft, while logically, Brady should have been the one getting the gift in this situation.

Being drafted in the sixth round and winning three Super Bowls makes Brady the highest return on investment in NFL history. Brady's lifetime pay up to that point was probably around $10 million, total. What possible leverage did Kraft have over Brady?

The next puzzling issue was the role of Brady's agent. Where was his mind when this act of grand larceny was occurring? No observer would believe that Tom Brady is a country bumpkin who could take or leave the money. Judging by his sense of style and taste in women, one can guess that he likes shiny things. He definitely wanted the money—hence his "frustration" with Kraft.

Tom Brady's agent is Don Yee. Don Yee represents Tom Brady, and no one else most fans have ever heard of. No agent should have allowed this inequity to occur.

The following will demonstrate how easily Tom Brady could have pocketed more money from the Patriots' vault.

1. Brady could fire Don Yee and hire Tom Condon, renowned NFL super-agent.

SPYGATE

2. Condon would remind Robert Kraft that the New England Patriots are the only team in the NFL that is named after a multi-state region, not a city. As such, the media market in New England is three or four times the size of Indianapolis or Atlanta, where Manning and Vick play football.

3. Condon would further remind Kraft that Jim Irsay, owner of the Colts, and Arthur Blank, owner of the Falcons, do not own their own stadiums, as Kraft does. Kraft had purchased the team in 1992 for $175 million; the team was then worth $1 billon (according to *Forbes* in 2005). These data points together mean that Brady's success on the field has improved Kraft's net wealth by many hundreds of millions of dollars. Ergo, Brady is worth much more to Kraft than Vick and Manning are to their teams' owners. Kraft needed to pay him or, naturally, Brady would want to be traded.

4. Brady should have rightfully been given a $20 million bonus based on work already done. As a sixth rounder draft choice, he was severely underpaid for all three Super Bowl titles. This contract was Kraft's chance to monetarily thank him.

It was clear that Brady had no need to sign that suspiciously inadequate contract. But he signed it, like a compliant employee. But the mystery remains as to why he surrendered so easily, and why Kraft was so adamant about not paying him.

As Peter King pointed out, in Brady's new 2005 contract he was to be paid about the same amount as Chad Pennington. King states this was intentionally done by Brady, who had been underpaid for all three Super Bowls, so the team would have more money left over for other players. That would only make logical sense if the Patriots were near the salary cap limit, which is almost never the case. From the 2001 to the 2005 seasons (the Super Bowl years), the Patriots' average NFL rank in salaries paid was #18. They were not even close to the salary cap limit, with ample room to pay more money to Brady if they wanted. They just didn't want to do it. Additionally, all parties involved knew that the salary cap was due to jump up significantly with the new TV network deal kicking in for the 2006 season. [4]

To say nothing of the fact that no other player in any team sport would ever be expected to adopt such an altruistic position, as to leaving $30 million on the negotiating table because he "gets it." Doesn't Brady have charities he would like to give money to as a donation?

In an apples-to-apples comparison, for the 2009 season, Tom Brady's base salary was $5 million. Peyton Manning's base salary was $14 million. Being four and five years into their new long-term deals, neither player had any signing bonus money paid for that year. As is typical, the New England Patriots were $21 million under the salary cap for the 2009 season. $10 million of that money could have easily gone to Tom Brady. The difference between what these two premier quarterbacks were paid was quite large and unexplainable.

In any case, teams always pay their superstars who deliver for the franchise at playoff time. The reason is financially motivated. Playoff teams sell out all their home games and luxury suites. Playoff contenders can ask for and receive big figures from local advertisers. Home playoff games bring additional revenue for everyone, and players' salaries are paid by the National Football League for these games.

SPYGATE

Only older players who are already wealthy, and trying to win that elusive Super Bowl ring, play for considerably less than market value. Brady was in the complete opposite situation—he had three rings on his hand and was nowhere near rich by NFL standards. Conversely he had made his owner a billionaire.

Brady was halfway through a career that could have ended in an instant with one horrific hit. This could have been his last best chance to hit a big payday. The average NFL career lasts a brief four years. NFL players have the worst contracts in the world of professional sports, with very little of their contract money guaranteed, compared to baseball and basketball players' contracts.

It appears highly likely that Belichick was essentially calling these shots, not Kraft. Although Scott Pioli was known as the Vice President of Player Personnel, he was never actually given the title of general manager for reasons only Bill Belichick knows. In a highly unusual move, Belichick was elevated from defensive coordinator with the Jets to director of all football operations in New England. Belichick himself retained all final veto power over player moves, which would naturally include contracts.

Some will argue that Robert Kraft is a shrewd businessman who would never shell out big money to any player. Given that theory as a backdrop, he would not be slighting Brady in this contract, just operating as usual—but all of that would be incorrect. When you look at the list of NFL quarterbacks who had landed $100 million contracts on or before the 2005 season, the names and figures will surprise you.

> Michael Vick, 10 years, $130 million
> Donovan McNabb, 12 years, $115 million
> Peyton Manning, 7 years, $98 million

BRYAN O'LEARY

> Brett Favre, 10 years, $100 million
> Carson Palmer, 10 years, $100 million
> Drew Bledsoe, 10 years, $102 million

The startling name here is Drew Bledsoe of the New England Patriots, the first quarterback in NFL history to sign a $100 million contract. Bledsoe had signed that monster deal before the 2000 season with none other than Robert Kraft. Kraft had made Bledsoe the highest paid quarterback in the NFL at that time. Ironically, he is the same Drew Bledsoe who could not win his job back from Tom Brady just one year later. Bledsoe and his contract were eventually shipped off to the Buffalo Bills.

Considering these amazing facts, it seems Kraft's behavior greatly changed by the 2005 season. How did Kraft go from spending like every other owner in the year 2000, to refusing to pay players' fair market value by the year 2005?

Spygate is what happened. With a new and improving sophisticated espionage system, the players were less important. The Spygate system made the team exceptional, and the offensive players were obviously the main beneficiaries of this system. Belichick, and naturally Brady, knew that Tom's performance was not entirely due to his own abilities. Brady is a top-notch quarterback no doubt, but he was getting a lot of help. Knowing your opponents' defense makes a quarterback's job much easier, as Steve Young stated earlier (pages 156-57).

Belichick and Brady shared this dark secret, a secret that was making them both look amazing. Kraft and Belichick knew Tom Brady was not going anywhere; this was the hidden leverage they had over Brady in the negotiations. And most likely why Brady does not have a big name agent, like other top NFL quarterbacks

SPYGATE

employ. This clearly indicates that the system is much more effective than fans have been led to believe. Otherwise, Brady should have walked away and landed a blockbuster contract of his own, somewhere else. Of course playing somewhere else would have been much harder for Brady, and he clearly didn't want that.

Naturally, they did not know it then, but they would be caught cheating a few years later, making this unfair contract easier to understand from an outsider's perspective. In hindsight it seems as though the Patriots still should have been somewhat more generous to Tom Brady. After all, he does throw a perfect spiral and cheating or not, somebody has to throw the passes. Nobody ever comes to Gillette Stadium to see Robert Kraft throw a deep out route.

But in these affairs of duplicity and chicanery, people always say: *follow the money*. And in this case the money flows to Bill Belichick and Robert Kraft, not the players. In this book's 2009 example, Manning was paid $14 million and Brady received $5 million, while Belichick managed to take home $7.5 million. Only in New England would "the best quarterback of all time" earn millions less than his coach.

Remember when Belichick was caught in the act of using the Spygate system at the Jets game in 2007, the incident that pulled back the curtain on their fraudulent deception? The first thing Kraft did, once Belichick and the team paid their fines to the NFL, was to give Belichick a contract extension and nearly double his salary. [5] Could their actions be any more obvious?

Endnotes

[1] McLuskey, Dex and Aaron Kuriloff. "NFL Signs Nine-Year Extensions of Television Contracts With CBS, FOX, NBC." *Bloomberg*, December 14, 2011. http://www.bloomberg.com/news/2011-12-14/nfl-renews-television-contracts-with-cbs-fox-nbc-networks-through-2022.html

[2] Badenhausen, Kurt, Michael K. Ozanian and Christina Settimi, eds. "Football's Most Valuable Teams." *Forbes*, September 7, 2011. http://www.forbes.com/lists/2011/30/nfl-valuations-11_land.html

[3] Pasquarelli, Len. "Brady Now Among the NFL's Highest-Paid Players." ESPN, May 8, 2005. http://sports.espn.go.com/nfl/columns/story?columnist=pasquarelli_len&id=2054072

[4] King, Peter. "Another Patriots Victory." *Sports Illustrated*, May 9, 2005. http://sportsillustrated.cnn.com/2005/writers/peter_king/05/08/mmqb.brady/

[5] Smith, Michael. "Sources: Patriots Give Belichick Long-Term Extension." ESPN, September 17, 2007. http://sports.espn.go.com/nfl/news/story?id=3023193

Statistical Anomalies

Section IV

Background for Statistical Analysis Chapters

Parity is the goal of the National Football League. Dynasties in the modern era of the National Football League should be nearly impossible, because the NFL is designed specifically to enhance parity. The NFL rules make life harder for good teams and easier for weak teams. The NFL does this to promote competition and a level playing field. More so than any other league, the NFL haves and have-nots are assisted as needed. At the beginning of each season, most every team has a chance at making the playoffs. Maybe the teams' chances are not identical, but they all have a shot. This is done by design, so that small market teams can play head to head with large market teams. This may be the reason the NFL has taken over fan interest as America's favorite pastime. No hard feelings, Twins fans, but few among us want to watch the New York Yankees beat up the Minnesota Twins.

The NFL has done a variety of clever things to promote parity. The NFL college draft is done in worst to best order. The teams having the most losses from the previous season choose first, working down through the order, with the Super Bowl winner choosing last. Moving from weakest to strongest allows the weakest NFL teams to get the best new college players each year. Other sports do this too, but the NFL does not stop there.

The NFL has a hard salary cap so that major market teams cannot outspend the small market teams for free agent talent. Large market Major League Baseball teams are well known for spending lavishly and acquiring many of the best players. This is a big advantage that large market teams have over smaller market teams in baseball.

SPYGATE

NFL free agency, which began in the early 90s, allows players to move unencumbered from team to team every couple of years. In the old days players were stuck in highly restrictive contracts, unable to move to another team for years. It was these restrictions that spawned dynastic teams like the Steelers and 49ers in the 70s and 80s. Those immortal teams could not be held together in today's NFL. With a salary cap and free agency, each year a successful team has very tough decisions to make about which players they can afford to keep, and which players to let slip through their fingers.

The NFL also does something entirely unique to pro football, unbeknownst to most fans. The NFL actually makes a team's schedule harder or easier based on how a team finished the previous season. Every year the NFL schedule makers place two games on each team's schedule in which the NFL will be matching teams who had the same standing in their respective divisions at last season's end. For example, if a team finished third in its division last season, it will play two games against teams who also finished third in their divisions last year (in the team's same conference, i.e. AFC). If a team played well last season and won its division, it will face two division winners on its schedule for the new season. The NFL does this to every team's schedule, just to make it harder or easier on each team. The sole purpose of this type of scheduling is to level the playing field, keep dynasties from forming, and promote parity.

If a team was lousy last season, then it will get two easier opponents on this year's schedule. Two games may not seem like a big deal; however, two games are thirteen percent of a sixteen-game schedule. Many teams miss the playoffs every year by only one loss. If a team is lucky enough to make the playoffs two years in a row, one loss can move them from the #1 seed to the #5 seed, meaning they likely will not be playing at home in the playoffs.

Imagine if Major League Baseball did something similar to this. To have the same effect, MLB rules would need to force the New York Yankees to play the Detroit Tigers and the Texas Rangers ten more games <u>each</u> in the 2012 season, based on all three teams winning their respective divisions the prior year. That equates to twenty more games against the top teams in baseball. Try winning three World Series titles under those rules, and one can understand why the formation of dynasties in the NFL should be a near impossibility.

Add to that, the NFL is a collision sport and that playoffs are single-game elimination. If a team loses one playoff game, its season is over. All of this gives ample support to observable evidence that winning NFL games in a highly consistent manner is very challenging.

To look for statistical footprints of the effectiveness of the Spygate system, a researcher would want to start with a few basic concepts. We know that the Patriots were caught, more than once, taping opponents' defensive signals with a hand-held camera. Pages 111-12 of this book detail the list of tapes turned over to the NFL by videographer Matt Walsh. The majority of these tapes record away games, not games at the Patriots' home stadium. When Belichick was asked directly by CBS reporter Armen Keteyian how many games Belichick had taped opponents' defensive signals, he answered without pause or need to collect his thoughts: "About half." [1]

At first, this seems like a very odd answer. Why half? If the Patriots were committed to cheating and it was working well, it seems questionable that they would only cheat in "about half" of their games. But Belichick does not exactly say that; he does not say he only cheated in half the games. Belichick said he has a man on the field holding a video camera pointed at defensive coaches during "about half" of the games. Then the reason became clear: Belichick's answer makes perfect sense because the other half of the Patriots' total games, they are playing a home game.

The Patriots would not need a sneaky employee with a cover story lurking on the sidelines if they are playing at their own stadium. They control the whole building; they could rig a hidden camera anywhere they wanted an eagle's eye view. A camera up in the booth with a telescopic lens would give them a close-up shot of anything on the sideline. In any team's home stadium, one can easily control communications devices and eavesdropping equipment. Bugging opponent's locker rooms would be child's play, if a team was that committed to cheating, which the Patriots have demonstrated.

If a hypothetical poker player suspected a rival player of cheating, and they thought this player was using a sophisticated surveillance system to find out what the other players' cards were; the last place opponents would want to play a poker tournament would be at their rival's home.

If true, the Patriots would be extremely difficult to beat at Gillette Stadium where they have complete control of the environment. Let us examine the Patriots' record in home games to see if there are any statistical anomalies. After all, football is a game of statistics. We can easily compare team performance against other teams of the past and present, to see if any irregularities are occurring. The population of NFL teams is so homogeneous that players move seamlessly from one team to another. All teams are playing by the same rules under the same conditions. NFL team performance should follow basic rules of statistical theory very closely.

Conducting the statistical analysis for this book is Dr. Miao Zang, who holds a PhD in Statistical Science from Southern Methodist University in Dallas, Texas. A Chinese national and fairly new to the USA, Dr. Zang was not aware of the Patriot's Spygate incident, making him an ideal unbiased, outside expert.

I asked Dr. Zang to study several statistical performance data points of National Football League teams. The idea of the study was to see if any team had any extreme performance that could not be considered "'normal'" for a game played by human beings that involves so much chance and variability, like professional football.

To keep this section of reasonable length, we chose the three data points that were most outstanding.

Home Game Win/Loss Record
Perfect Home Record
Record Against The Spread (Vegas Betting Lines)

SPYGATE

Endnotes

[1] Belichick, Bill. "Eye to Eye: Bill Belichick," interview by Armen Keteyian, CBS News, September 20, 2007. http://www.youtube.com/watch?v=Hyg9BhqESxU

Home Game Records

Chapter 10

For a team to perform well at their home stadium is not odd or suspicious. Many NFL teams are very good when playing in their home stadiums. Just winning games does not make a team guilty of cheating. But there is a difference between playing well and playing suspiciously well.

If the Patriots were truly gaining a meaningful advantage by using the Spygate system, that advantage should show up in a study of this kind.

---

by Miao Zang PhD Statistical Science
Part I: Study of Win/Loss Records at Home

For a statistical study of the New England Patriots win/loss record when playing at home, in **Figure 1** we see a scatter plot of average number of home wins, per season, for each team in

SPYGATE

the NFL from 2001 to 2011. Every team in the NFL is represented by solid dots, while the New England Patriots are represented by a solid triangle.

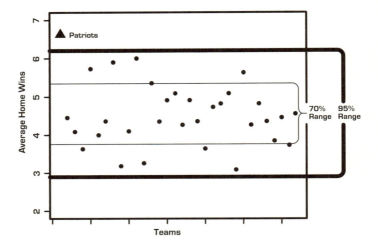

Figure 1: Scatter plot of average home wins of 32 teams from 2001 to 2011. The solid triangle is the New England Patriots; the two thicker solid lines refer to the 95% range; the two thinner solid lines refer to the 70% range.

The average number of home wins of an NFL teams is 4.55 games, out of 8 home games played, with a standard deviation of .84 games. The average NFL team wins a little more than half its home games each season. A standard deviation is a statistical measurement which tells us how much each team's performance differs (or deviates) from the average. A low standard deviation of .84 games (less than 1 game) tells us the population of NFL teams is made up of members who perform very similarly to one another.

From a purely statistical analysis we would expect that approximately 70% of all NFL teams have an average wins per season in the range of 3.71 to 5.39 (4.55 plus or minus the standard deviation .84), which is referenced by the two thin lines in the scatter plot: **70% confidence range**. The actual fact is that 69% of 32 teams fall in the range of 3.71 to 5.39. So far, observed performance fits statistical predictions.

Now let us move two standard deviations away from the average, which results in the **95% confidence range** of 2.87 to 6.23, equating 4.55 plus or minus (2 x .84) (two standard deviations).

In statistical theory, this range is expected to cover all the "reasonable" members of the population. Any number outside this 95% range is considered to be an "unreasonable" member of the population, an outlier. It could be due to some factors other than randomness or because this member, for some reason, does not belong to this population. In **Figure 1**, the range of 2.87 to 6.23 is referenced by the two thick lines. We can see that this range covers all NFL teams except for the New England Patriots; they are outside that band. At nearly 7 wins per season, they are nearly 3 standard deviations away from the average, an extreme outlier.

One should not view 95% confidence, as meaning 5% of all teams will fall outside the 95% confidence band. In fact, we should almost never see any members of a homogeneous population, like NFL teams made up of the same players, fall outside the 95% confidence range. As a statistical scientist, I would normally examine or question: "What makes this member so different from the others?" "Is there a non-football related reason why their performance is such an anomaly?" "Is it due to

SPYGATE

the extremely cold weather in Boston that gives the Patriots an advantage when playing at home?"

Figure 2 is a histogram of average number of home wins per season over those same 11 years. A histogram will show us groupings of different outcomes.

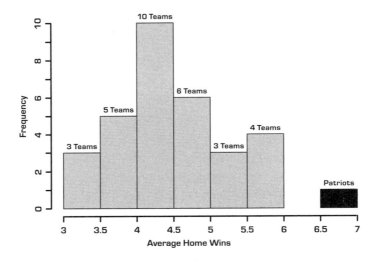

Figure 2: Histogram of average home wins from 2001 to 2011.

We bin the frequency of outcomes, so that we can see the distribution of these outcomes, in other words, how many NFL teams won a given number of games in each bin per year. For example, three teams won between 3 games and 3.5 home games per season, and the number of teams who won between 4 and 4.5 games is 10. You can see that the distribution is symmetric and bell shaped. In statistical theory, this is the exact shape of a distribution of random averages if they are from the same homogeneous population (like NFL Teams). Meanwhile, this shape also validates the analysis in the previous paragraph. In statistical theory, all members of a similar statistical population should fall within a 95% confidence range. It is striking to me that zero NFL teams average 6-6.5 wins per season. Yet somehow, there is New England all the way out near 7 wins. That is, they average nearly 7 home wins per year, out of 8 home games played for eleven years and an extreme performance to say the least.

By my statistical calculation, the odds of having a better average home record than the New England Patriots over this 11-year period is .67% which is 1/150. In any other study of like populations I would be trying to eliminate this outlier as "not a member" of this population, as their performance is too extreme. It is technically possible as "anything is possible" but highly unlikely in a study of this nature. In statistical sense, the New England Patriots' 6.64 wins per season over 11 years is significantly different from the level which should be achievable by an NFL team, given the homogenous nature of NFL teams as a population.

The most striking aspect of this analysis, and one that shocked us, is that when viewing the pre-2007 cheating statistics (admitted to by the Patriots) and comparing them to the post-2007 performance, when the Patriots say they stopped cheating, the team's performance is just as good or better. This can only mean one of two things.

One: The cheating system had no material effect on the Patriots' performance, as most fans and media members have been led to believe.

SPYGATE

Or two: The Patriots never stopped using some kind of system and continued to employ methods that gave the team an advantage. First, observe all of the statistical evidence, then come to your own conclusions on this delicate subject.

As Dr. Zang's analysis shows, the New England Patriots are an extreme anomaly when it comes to winning home games at Gillette Stadium. For a team to perform well does not explain their near-perfection. New England has somehow managed to take normal variability of performance out of their home games. They are machine-like in their ability to win at home.

Since the Patriots were averaging nearly seven wins out of eight games per year, we decided to study perfection. A perfect home season is eight wins and zero losses. Perfection in life—and the NFL—is rare.

Perfect at Home

Chapter 11

Playing well at home is one thing, but playing perfectly at home is something else entirely. An NFL season is sixteen games: eight at home and eight played on the road. How rare is it for an NFL team to complete a perfect 8-0 home game season? Take these facts into consideration; the Dallas Cowboys, led by Troy Aikman, never had a single season where they went 8-0 at home, at Texas Stadium. The Indianapolis Colts, led by Peyton Manning, have been perfect at home only one time in fourteen seasons. The St. Louis Rams teams with Kurt Warner, known as the "Greatest Show on Turf" for their home turf wizardry, were also 8-0 at home only one time.

In fact, over the twenty years of true free agency in the NFL, dating back to 1990, nearly half of the NFL teams have never had an 8-0 home season, not once. Given these statistics, "perfect" in the NFL is very difficult to accomplish. *On any given Sunday* is the famous football phrase that means that any NFL team can beat any other NFL team "on any given Sunday." A stark reminder

SPYGATE

of this fact occurred this season in 2011. An absolute lock to finish the 2011 season with a perfect 16-0 record, the Green Bay Packers lost their shot at perfection by losing to the Kansas City Chiefs. That Sunday the Chiefs started a third-string quarterback and featured a head coach who had been fired and replaced. Yet somehow, the Chiefs managed to beat the best team in the NFL at that moment. Perfection in today's NFL is nearly impossible.

---

by Miao Zang PhD Statistical Science
Part II: Study of Perfect Home Seasons

"Perfect home season" means that in a regular season, a team wins all eight home games (8-0). From 2001 to 2011, there are a total of nineteen occurrences in the National Football League. Ten teams had one perfect home season. The Green Bay Packers, Seattle Seahawks and New England Patriots achieved a perfect home season more than one time.

Since there are a total of 32 teams in the National Football League and the period of interest is 11 years, the total number of seasons is 32 (teams) multiplied by 11 (seasons), which is 352 seasons. In these 352 seasons, nineteen of them are perfect, 8-0. Therefore, the probability (or chance) for any team to have a perfect home season is estimated to be 5.4% (19/352). Let us put the situation this way: a team (any team) has 5.4% chance to get perfect home in each season and it will try 11 seasons. Think of a gambling example: in each bet you have a 5.4% chance to win. If you keep playing 11 times, how many times can you win?

Perhaps zero. In fact, your chance of zero occurrences of an 8-0 seasons is 54%. This is the same question as our case. In Statistics, this kind of question is called a binomial question. You are perfect or you are not. After statistical calculations, the chances of all possible outcomes are listed in **Table 1**.

Outcome (11 seasons)	Chance (probability)
0 perfect home seasons	54%
1 perfect home season	34%
2 perfect home seasons	10%
3 perfect home seasons	1.7%
4 perfect home seasons	0.19%
5 perfect home seasons	.15% or 1 in 7000
6 perfect home seasons	1 in 115,000
7 perfect home seasons	1 in 2.8 million
8 perfect home seasons	almost 0

Table 1: Chances of all possible outcomes of binomial question.

As a team attempts to get more and more perfect home seasons, this corresponding chance is getting smaller and smaller. From the **Table 1**, we can also see that it is almost impossible to get more than seven perfect home seasons, based on this study.

There is 54% chances to get no perfect home season in 11 years. Therefore, of the 32 teams of the National Football League according to statistical theory, 54% x 32 = 18 teams are expected to get zero perfect home seasons, and the observed facts are 19 of them achieved no perfect home season.

SPYGATE

The observed facts are very close to the predicted outcome. Similarly, according to statistical theory, we expect to see about 34% x 32 = 11 teams get only one perfect home season. The observed fact is that 10 teams got only one perfect home season. Moreover, the expected number of teams to get two perfect home seasons is 10% x 32 = 3, and we see two teams got two perfect home seasons. All those predicted numbers are very close to the true numbers. Let us have a look at the New England Patriots case. The New England Patriots have had five perfect home seasons over 11 years. The chance of getting five perfect home seasons is 0.015% (1/7000). Therefore, we expect 0.005 (0.015% x 32) teams can achieve this mark. That is an extreme anomaly. Let us consider these numbers in the opposite way; 1/7000 also means that if 7,000 teams try 11 years, we expect to see only one team can achieve this mark. However, the New England Patriots made it in a league with 32 teams. In a statistical sense, based on the fact that there are 19 occurrences of perfect home seasons in the past 11 years, the event that the New England Patriots had five perfect home seasons from 2001 to 2011 is statistically highly unusual and deserves inspection. If most teams cannot complete a perfect home season even one time, how can New England do this over and over five times? What makes this extreme home game advantage occur?

At first glance, a one in 7,000 chance of having five perfect home seasons might not seem that far-fetched, until you realize that your odds are better of giving birth to an NFL football player.

Provided you have a boy and he plays high school football. You see, a high school football player has a one in 6,000 chance of playing in the NFL. Your odds of dying by electrocution are one in 6,000. Either way, the chance is possible but extremely rare. These are the odds of something occurring out of a population of millions. Now imagine you are in a room with only 32 people; chances that any of them will be parents of an NFL player are next to none. These things should not happen in very small populations that are homogeneous.

Here is a logical question: if the Patriots can win all 8 home games, can they keep on winning 12 home games in a row, picking up the following season? Perfect means they win every game at home. How about 20 games in a row at home? No, that would be impossible. Everything would have to go the team's way; every referee's call, every tipped pass, injuries, the weather. There are too many variables to mention. There are simply too many factors, including too much luck, involved in sports to allow for that many consecutive wins.

In the last twenty years, 47% of NFL teams have never had an 8-0 home season. Yet somehow, the Patriots led by Tom Brady have accomplished this over and over—in twenty years of trying, nearly half of the other NFL teams could not do even one time!

Aside from the 2008 season, which Brady did not play due to injury, the New England Patriots led by Tom Brady have an eyebrow-raising official NFL record of winning 31 consecutive regular season home games. To repeat, that's 31 home wins in a row!

They demolished the previous NFL record by nearly an entire season. That is a breathtaking four straight seasons without a single home loss. Does that sound like the kind of NFL football you watch your favorite team play on Sunday?

SPYGATE

Every fan has been there. You know the game, when your team is winning all day, and the game goes down to the wire. Just when you thought you had won, as the final seconds tick away the other team snatches the victory from your win column.

Your team just lost a home game you were sure they would win. That scenario never happens in New England; the Patriots rack up home wins as though they are preordained. The Patriots mow down home opponents like they were playing the Big East, scheduled just to pad their win/loss record.

> **MIT Challenge:**
> To any and all statistics students and professors at MIT, please calculate the odds of winning 31 home games in a row when nearly half of a given population has not ever won 8 games in a row.

How is this level of consistent winning possible in a league built on parity? Are the Patriots "just that good"? The pundits will say the Patriots are "just that good at home." But who are the "the Patriots"?

From the first game of the 31-game win streak, to the last game of the streak, only 5 Patriots players played in all those games. Nearly the entire team roster turned over, to say nothing of all the coaching changes. So observers are supposed to believe the best team in NFL history by far, is anyone wearing a Patriots uniform, playing a home game in Gillette Stadium?

Brady, Belichick, and Ernie Adams are the constants, and they are clearly doing something that removes nearly all the normal variability of team performance in their home games. This performance level should be impossible if they are playing the same game by the same rules the other NFL teams are playing.

Five perfect home seasons means that in the last 21 years, Tom Brady is a better home game quarterback than:

        Troy Aikman (0)   Peyton Manning (1)
        Kurt Warner (1)   Dan Marino (0)
        Jim Kelly (1)   Drew Brees (1)
        [1990-2011 records]

Tom Brady has more 8-0 perfect home seasons than all these current and future Hall of Famers <u>combined</u>. This breathtaking performance crosses from impressive into unreasonably good territory.

The only quarterback and team to come close to this amazing record of perfect home seasons serves as a useful example of studying statistical outliers. The John Elway led Denver Broncos of the late 90s had three 8-0 perfect home seasons. They are the only other NFL quarterback and team in the last twenty years to have more than two perfect home seasons. Some "teams" have accomplished three perfect home seasons over the span of twenty years, but they did so with completely different players spaced many years apart. And while the Denver Broncos weren't cheating, they were getting some non-football help from the home environment. The high altitude in Denver saps the strength of opposing team's players, giving the altitude conditioned Broncos players a very real advantage. That extra edge turned a very good Denver Broncos team into an 8-0 perfect-at-home Broncos team. As this example shows, when you see a statistical outlier an observer should ask, "What's going on here? Why is this performance so outstanding?" And sure enough, you find the answer: altitude. No one is suggesting that New England does not have a very good football team, but being very good is a lot different than being perfect.

Hypothetically, consider if the world record for the 100 meter dash was broken by an eighteen-year-old kid who ran the race in five seconds. Should we congratulate him, or ask him "How far is Krypton from here, exactly?" Superhuman feats can only be acknowledged so far until they become truly unbelievable.

Against The Spread

Chapter 12

Anyone who has ever been to Las Vegas knows that games of chance are devised so that the house wins more than it loses. After all, Las Vegas was not built by fools. The big casinos spend millions of dollars watching for players who are winning in ways that should be impossible. If a player rolls craps for two hours without losing, the house does not hand the player a trophy, they show the player to a private room with very large men waiting. Those men will give the player a heart to heart discussion on the laws of probability and chance. They may even work in a few lessons on the laws of gravity. In short, the house identifies a cheater by those who are winning too often.

National Football League wagering in the USA is a gigantic business. On football games, over $7 billion is wagered each week, and nearly $9 billion is wagered on the Super Bowl game each year. To bet on a football game, you can simply choose the team you think will win, and then get paid if you are right. A bet of that nature is called the "money line" bet.

But that is not the way most gamblers bet on football games. The most common way to bet on football uses what is called the spread or line. A line will be expressed like this:

DALLAS -3 Arizona
Dallas is favored in this game. The capital letters means Dallas is playing at home. If you want to bet on Dallas you have to "give up" three points to the house. This means Dallas must win by more than three points for you to win your bet. To be declared the winner and collect your money, Dallas must "cover" the three points you gave the house when placing the bet. Any close game (under 3 points) or an outright win by the underdog Arizona Cardinals results in you losing the bet. If Dallas were to win by exactly 3, the bet is a tie and your bet is returned.

The professionals setting the lines in Vegas use part science, part art. They start with known variables like defensive and offensive strength versus opponents, recent performance, injuries, a team's record on grass verses artificial turf, etc. Then the major sports books post the lines to fine-tune their collective intelligence, essentially comparing notes. Their aim is to predict the score of each matchup as accurately as possible.

However, the ultimate goal of the house is to get approximately the same amount of money wagered on each team in every game. This is the goal, because the sports books charge a 10% "vigorish" on losing bets, while winning bets are paid off with even money. If you want to bet $100 on a game, you either win $100 or lose $110. If half of the bets are placed on the favorite, and half are placed on the underdog, the house makes money every game. The winners are paid by the losers' wagers and the house nets the 10% vig at zero risk.

What this means to the bettor is important; a line may start with a prediction of point differential, but it will move in order to entice bettors to place money on the underdog. The resulting line makes the favored team's line even harder for that team to cover. The bookies are essentially bribing bettors to even out their wagering book. Good teams who cover the spread consistently are bad news for Las Vegas sports books because this is where all the public money is bet. Non-professional gamblers love favorites. If there is an imbalance of betting money, it is usually on the favorite side of each game.

A team using a cheating system would be winning in unpredictable ways that could not be accounted for by the professionals setting the Vegas lines. The core of a betting line is known variables, but what of unknown variables like the highly effective Spygate system? Even non-football variables like the altitude in Denver can be accounted for, if one can prove that advantage exists. However, if the secret Spygate system was giving the Patriots an advantage and altering the score of the game, then the Patriots should have margins of victory that are beyond what was predicted. Said another way, the Patriots would have a very good record of winning games, Against The Spread (ATS).

It is one thing to beat the Arizona Cardinals on the field; it is quite another to beat the house in Las Vegas. It is important to note that a very good team can still have a weak record against the spread. A team could win most every game but not cover the spread very often. Good teams naturally face large point spreads.

SPYGATE

> For this study we used team's performance against the spread as reported by three sources: SportsRumble, BangtheBook, and BetVegas websites. When all three did not agree, we used the numbers two sources agreed on. The outcome of the study was not altered by the differences is these various sources.

by Miao Zang PhD Statistical Science
Part III: Against The Spread Analysis (Regular Season Only)

Let us look at the histogram of team performance against the spread for eleven seasons from 2001 to 2011. The distributions of wins against the betting lines (covers) of all NFL teams are in **Figure 3**.

The center is close to zero, indicating that most teams win and lose around 50/50 against the spread, and the distribution is also symmetric and bell shaped. This assures us that this analysis follows basic statistical rules of a population study. All numbers are expressed as net numbers (93 wins with 80 losses nets 13 winning bets).

The Patriots have won 105 games and lost 67 games (6 ties) against the spread for an amazing +38 net winning bets. By winning 38 net games, the Patriots are once again nearly three standard deviations away from the league average. After calculations, the average ATS of all NFL teams is 0.34 and the standard deviation of 13.18.

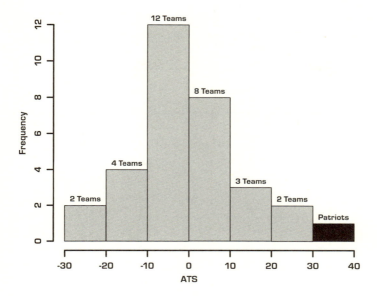

Figure 3: Histogram of ATS from 2001 to 2011.

This makes the Patriots an extremely rare case in a statistical sense.

In **Figure 4** we can see that the 70% range, which is represented by the two thin lines in the middle, covers 75% (25 teams) of all NFL teams. The 95% range is represented by the two thick lines and covers almost all NFL teams except the Patriots and the Rams (the very bottom dot). This indicates that the Patriots' margin of victory is quite often better than Vegas betting lines were predicting. The average NFL performance against the spread being so close to zero indicates that generally speaking, the Vegas spreads are very close to the true outcomes. Except in the case of the New England Patriots; their ATS +38 is almost three standard deviations away from the average 0.34. That means the ATS of the Patriots is an extreme outlier in a statistical sense.

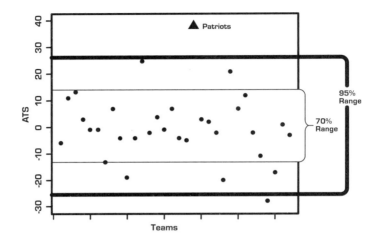

Figure 4: Scatter plot of ATS of 32 teams from 2001 to 2011. The solid triangle is the New England Patriots; the two thicker, solid lines refer to the 95% range; the two thinner solid lines refer to the 70% range.

It should be noted that against the spread and home win loss records, measured earlier, have little relationship to one another. Why is that? Firstly, this ATS study is measuring home <u>and away games</u>, effectively doubling the measured data sample. Secondly, the Vegas lines are adjusted higher to give the Patriots' opponents more points when they are playing at the Patriots' home field. The New England Patriots' ability to play especially well at home is a known fact to bettors and Vegas line setters. Once again a different data point leads to the New England Patriots being an extreme outlier—interesting.

To get expert commentary on the against the spread results, I turned to the foremost authority on gambling and sports betting in the USA.

Wayne Allyn Root is the most honored sports gambling prognosticator in the world. He has been selling his services to sports bettors for over twenty-five years.

His books include:

Betting to Win on Sports
The Zen of Gambling: the Ultimate Guide to Risking It All
The King of Vegas' Guide to Gambling

Read what others have written about Wayne Root.

"Wayne's the king of handicappers...he's the Warren Buffett of his world."—James J. Cramer, CNBC Host of *Mad Money*

"Wayne Allyn Root is The Face of Las Vegas Gaming.... [Wayne] has built a talent for picking football winners into a TV sports prognosticating empire."—*Las Vegas Sun*

"Wayne Allyn Root is perhaps the leading sports handicapper in the country.... Root has made a fortune...with a business that looks and feels like a brokerage house, Vegas-style. It's Wall Street versus *Wayne's Street!*"—CNBC Profile on Wayne Allyn Root

SPYGATE

"The Odds King of Las Vegas."—Bill Griffith, CNBC Host

"Wayne Allyn Root is an American gambling legend."—John O'Reilly, Managing Director Ladbrokes.com, the World's Largest Legal Bookmaker

"The Benjamin Graham of Gambling."—*Fortune Magazine*

My interview with Wayne Allyn Root occurred on January 25, 2012:

O'Leary: Why is it difficult for good teams to consistently beat the spread?

Root: If they [sports books] don't add more points to an underdog's line, they can't get enough people to take that underdog and even out the betting. People are afraid of underdogs, which is why the average NFL team doesn't win more against the spread, the lines are too high. They [NFL teams] cannot beat the adjusted spreads on a regular basis. That makes underdogs a great bet for the bettor, as they are getting more points than they should. Some lines seem reasonable to both sides and very small lines don't move very much.

O'Leary: What factors are taken into consideration when setting the spreads?

Root: The line setters argue amongst themselves about strength of defense, a team's performance on grass versus artificial turf, recent wins, coaching, etc. As a team wins and covers one week, they are adjusted up each week. If the line starts at -7, public perception might bump it up to -8.5.

O'Leary: The Patriots have been beating the Vegas line by an average of 3.5 games per year over the last eleven years. They are +38 games during that span of time. Have you ever seen any team consistently beat the bookies like this?

Root: No, it should be impossible. Not in my lifetime. Maybe back in the 50's, Packers and Colts era.

O'Leary: How long have you been picking games for clients? When you say, not in my lifetime, what does that mean?

Root: I have been in this business for over 26 years.

O'Leary: Were you aware that the Patriots had such an amazing record of beating the spreads?

Root: I have lost a lot of money in my life betting against Brady. We knew we were getting beat by the guys in Boston. I knew that when I bet against Brady, I have been beat a lot, but I didn't know it was that bad.

O'Leary: How is it that you were not aware of these statistics?

Root: Because my business moves too fast, the teams change every year, what they [Patriots] did three years ago has no bearing on my pick next week. You see what I mean, I don't have any use for ten years of data.

O'Leary: Why is this kind of success against the betting line so hard to believe; why should it be impossible?

Root: Theoretically, odds makers are supposed to take that into account, when a team is beating spreads. If the public is always betting on New England, the spreads should have been jacked up to counteract that [making spreads even higher] so it's surprising to hear that it was that high [number of covers], wow, unbelievable. It could be some of the cheating.

O'Leary: Have you ever seen this many covered bets in any other sport?

Root: No, I have not.

O'Leary: When you heard about the Spygate system in 2007, did you think back on all the bets you lost against the Patriots and say, "That's how the Patriots were killing us! They were cheating!"

Root: I have always been a New York cynical guy but I guess I am being a little naive on this one; if people asked me, "Is this cheating?" I would say, "No it's not, Brady is just great, Belichick is just great." But now that I look at the numbers, we've proven they have cheated [Spygate incident] and I guess they could be still doing it. Historically we have not seen this [consistently beating spreads] ever.

O'Leary: Do you want to go on the record with your Super Bowl pick this year?

Root: Never in history have we had a Super Bowl team with such a crappy defense [Patriots]. They [Patriots] had the worst defense in football and somehow they went 7-1 at home. The Giants are the pick; they have a much better defense and are getting points. I did the same with the New Orleans Saints over the Indianapolis Colts two years ago and my clients won a lot of money. The better defense usually wins in big postseason games. I am going with the Giants, but now you are making me nervous. (Laughing)

His title is well deserved; The King of Prognosticators was right, again!

As Mr. Root accurately points out, the Patriots' performance against the spread is the most damning. How can the betting lines be so accurate for almost every other team except New England, who sits at a bookie busting +38 games

SPYGATE

over eleven years? If you haven't gotten your money's worth of enjoyment out of this book, at least now you have a good chance to make some big money. Armed with the knowledge that New England wins 61% of all their regular season games against the spread, placing money on them in a home game seems like a good bet.

Conclusion

By now, you might be wondering who I am and why I have written this book. But first, I want to thank you for taking the time to read *Spygate: The Untold Story*.

I am an NFL fan like you. A soccer dad from the Southwest with three little girls and a wife so amazing my friends keep telling me that I have out-kicked my coverage. I am truly very blessed in many ways.

Living in a household with divided NFL loyalty is exciting. It is not uncommon in the Dallas suburbs, as many transplants have moved here and married the natives. My wife is a diehard Cowboys fan, having grown up in Pasadena, Texas. Every weekend during the football season I have to hear about the wonderful Jason Witten, and how Tony Romo makes her want to pull her hair out.

On the other hand, I hail from the small town of Bellevue just outside of Pittsburgh, Pennsylvania and was raised a Steelers fan. As a Steelers fan, I have had more than my fair share of NFL nirvana moments. I love the NFL and always have since I was a child. Four Lombardis in six years will do that to a kid. The NFL is like no other sport. It is America's favorite spectator sport for good reason. The players are like modern-day gladiators. It is a perfect combination of artistic expression and brute force, with an added element of strategy that is second to none.

This book is not a hit job on any player or team. The true subject of this book is the institutional and societal acceptance of cheating as a way to gain a competitive advantage. As a father of three young girls who play sports, my wife and I use the lessons of these games as teaching tools to enforce values that we want to impress on our children. Principles include fair play, sportsmanship, and losing with grace. The most important and first lesson every child learns is to play by the rules.

When the New England Patriots coaches and staff created and perfected a cheating system that allowed them to defraud the other teams in the NFL, they cheated all of us. As fans we pour our heart and soul into our team's successes and failures. Many times your Monday mood can be greatly influenced by the outcome of your favorite team's Sunday game. The concept that some of these games could have been influenced more by what is being done off the field, than on it, changes the basic tenets of the game itself. A football game is not a football game when your opponent knows what you're going to do next. Institutionalized cheating has no place in our national pastime.

Over the past four years since the Spygate story first occurred at the Jets game in 2007, I have had conversations with other diehard NFL fans all over the USA. In my real job, I travel all over the country. When the subject of Spygate comes up, the most often heard phrase is this one: "I can't believe the Patriots got a pass on that!" How do we know how good a player is, how smart a coach is, or what team is a dynasty, if cheating played a significant role in their success? The feeling is unshakable; every Sunday we have ex-NFL players telling us about a genius coach and a certain player who is a "first ballot Hall-of-Famer." But in the back of your mind, you're left thinking, "Are they, really?"

When I started doing a little research on this subject, I was actually shocked that there wasn't already a book written on the Spygate controversy. It has everything: sex, lies, and videotape. Well, maybe no sex, but NFL action is the next best thing for most guys. Add to that, what seems to be a cover-up from the top of the league, all the way through the complicit sports media. As I dug for more information, I was stunned by the mountain of evidence stacked against the three-time Super Bowl winners.

The saying goes: *For evil to prosper, all that it takes is for good men to do nothing.*

As you can imagine, being a fan, I had no access to the principals in this case. No matter, they would not have spoken to me anyway, with the cover-up still in full effect. Nevertheless, the evidence speaks for itself. People have an amazing ability to know the truth when they hear it.

- The NFL investigative effort in this case is curious at best.
- Testimony from ex-players, coaches, and a videographer, all stating that the Spygate system was used to great effect
- Mysterious responsibilities of a hidden mastermind, Ernie Adams
- Bizarre coach-hiring practices at Patriots' headquarters
- The unexplainable grossly undercompensated Tom Brady
- Josh McDaniels' own words and actions
- Statistics of near impossible performance, especially concerning against the spread

Individually, maybe these data points can be explained—but as a mosaic the facts are hard to ignore. There should be no controversy that the evidence is clear, the only controversy seems to be: why is the public left under mass hypnosis?

This book's version of events matches what we actually saw and what occurred. The official version "for public consumption," the version the NFL has been pushing through the media, does not.

SPYGATE

There is absolutely no way we can ever know how good the Patriots really would have been without these clear advantages. If the Spygate system did not help them, why did they devote so much energy into perfecting it? Everyone who looked into the matter had a strong reason to marginalize the event and tell us that it didn't somehow affect the outcome of these games.

The statistical analysis of several data points shows they are winning in ways that should not be possible, before and after 2007. No team in NFL history has come close to this level of performance.

Who is ensuring that this is not continuing to occur in some way? Roger Goodell? Consider the lengthy profile of Roger Goodell, revealed by *Sports Illustrated*'s Peter King.

Goodell explained to King that as part of Belichick's punishment for illegally spying, the three-time Super Bowl winning coach had to issue an apology. "I was given assurances that [Belichick] would tell his side of the story," Goodell said. "He went out and stonewalled the press. I feel like I was deceived." [1]

So, instead of fining Belichick additional money or suspending him for not complying, Goodell complained to reporter Peter King four years later? Roger Goodell is on the record categorically stating that Belichick intentionally used a cheating system. Goodell stated: "I think I'm pretty well on the record here. I didn't accept Bill Belichick's explanation for what happened and I still don't to this day." [2]

If you think the Patriots "wouldn't dare" do it again, consider that they were warned to stop cheating, by letter in 2006, and then continued cheating anyway. Josh McDaniels, a key figure in both Spygate incidents (caught and punished spying) is still coaching in New England today.

Addressing all sports reporters: Fans would like you to ask these simple questions:

Ask Belichick what Ernie Adams does on game day.

Ask Teddy Bruschi if he was ever given a list of an opposing quarterback's audibles. Did that help him on Super Bowl Sunday?

Ask Tom Brady if he ever got defensive formations spoken into his helmet after the 15-second cutoff, especially during a Super Bowl.

With the strong support of Robert Kraft, Roger Goodell just received a contract extension through the 2018 season. His pay is said to be doubling from $10 million per season this year to nearly $20 million per season. [3] Goodell seems to have done everything he can to protect the NFL.

What does all this mean to the average fan? It depends on who you ask. I was having a conversation recently with a lifelong friend, Bill O'Connor. Bill is a forty-year season ticket holder in Pittsburgh. In his opinion Spygate was not a big deal, because at the end of the day, the players have to make the plays. He continued that it probably gave the Patriots a three-point per game advantage. Many share this opinion and I can understand why. After all, Wes Welker still has to beat his man and Tom Brady has to throw a good pass to score a touchdown. It's not as though any defensive formation will leave a receiver uncovered. The issue boils down to the fact that the players must actually play the game and I understand that opinion.

SPYGATE

In truth, the stolen plays may have only helped the Patriots on only a few important plays per game. The problem is that the three points per game that Bill O'Connor is estimating the Patriots gained is all the help they would need in today's NFL. For the seven years of cheating that the Patriots have already admitted (2000 – 2006), the Patriots won twenty games by three points or less. Those twenty games include three playoff games and all three Super Bowls. Take away three points per game and those Patriot Super Bowl wins are at risk.

The margin of victory in the NFL is razor-thin and the statistics show the Patriots' coin flip always lands heads up. 7,000 to 1 are the odds of having five 8-0 home seasons in eleven seasons, the same as the odds of getting struck by lightning in one lifetime.

If it was not worth three points a game, why would the entire coaching staff "practice, coach it, and work on it," as longtime Patriots coach Josh McDaniels admitted to his staff in Denver.

This book is for clear-thinking people who have, up until now, not been getting all of the actual facts about this case. As you have read here, this Spygate scandal was largely ignored by the media and severely underreported. This is not just a case about a football team—this incident is about who we are as a society. Where do you draw the line?

In the past I was always impressed by the Patriots, their team-first attitude, never paid big money to free agents, they were always far below the salary cap and yet were still a successful team. Then they were caught cheating and it all made sense to me—*that's how they were doing it!*

But then a strange thing happened—nobody cared.

I cannot understand how people can keep talking about dynasty and team of the decade, and model franchise, as though cheating is acceptable, that it did not matter anyway. It matters to me and a lot of other fans, too.

What Barry Bonds did does not compare to what the Patriots did to the other NFL teams. What the Patriots did was at the management level and seems to be all but ignored by the league, so that we, the fans, would not think the games and Lombardi trophies were tainted. This Spygate affair is the biggest cheating scandal in American sports history. It overshadows the Black Sox throwing the World Series in 1919. At least the Black Sox conspired to actually lose the Series. The Patriots conspired to win, and won three Super Bowls.

In 2007 the Patriots were not only winning, they were running no-huddle sets and throwing 50-yard touchdown passes when they were already winning the game by 30 points. Adding insult to injury, the NFL found it critical that the Patriots were successful in 2007 to support the cover story. *See, they still win without cheating!*

You never see hour-long specials on the greatness of Barry Bonds, because we know he cheated. Even though, for most of Bonds' career, he was an amazing talent who did not take performance enhancing drugs. But facts are facts. And the facts are, he blew up his body with chemicals and broke some very important hitting records. Most folks feel his records should carry an asterisk.

Hall of Fame coach Don Shula stated the following:

"I guess you got the same thing as putting an asterisk by Barry Bonds' home run record. Belichick was fined $500,000, the team was fined $250,000 and they lost a first-round draft choice. That tells you the seriousness or significance of what they found." [4] I could not agree more with this sentiment.

SPYGATE

Shula continued, "The Spygate thing has diminished what they've accomplished. You would hate to have that attached to your accomplishments. They've got it." [4]

I guess in the end it is up to people like us, the fans, to make sure the asterisk stays firmly planted and not wiped away by people who are paid by the NFL to cover up this sad event. My hope is that this book will be a conversation starter. As fans, you and I are free to have our own opinions about what the Patriots did to the rest of the National Football League and what their legacy should be.

We, the people get to determine what we believe and what we accept as facts. That's what this country is all about. They say that sunshine is the best antiseptic. So with this book, let the sunshine in!

Once again, I thank you for your time, and the best of luck to you and your team. This book is for people who think that games should be played by the rules or not at all.

Bryan

www.Spygatebook.com

Join the conversation on Twitter: #Spygate

Endnotes

[1] King, Peter. "The Man of the Hour." *Sports Illustrated*, February 7, 2011. http://sportsillustrated.cnn.com/vault/article/magazine/MAG1181467/index.htm

[2] Reiss, Mike. "Patriots Never Taped Walkthrough, Goodell Finds." *Boston Globe*, May 14, 2008. http://articles.boston.com/2008-05-14/sports/29274687_1_roger-goodell-tape-videotaping

[3] Brinson, Will. "Report: Goodell's Salary to 'Double' Up to $20M." CBS Sports, February 13, 2012. http://www.cbssports.com/mcc/blogs/entry/22475988/34822324

[4] Myers, Gary. "Don Shula: Spygate Would Mar Pats' Undefeated Season." *New York Daily News*, November 6, 2007. http://www.nydailynews.com/sports/football/don-shula-spygate-mar-pats-undefeated-season-article-1.255721

Acknowledgements

Foremost, I want to thank Jesus Christ, the Prince of Peace. I really must thank my dearest wife Paula, for her love and support in all that I do. Much thanks to my brothers Dan the man, Rick, and sister Beth Ann for all of their good humor and encouragement. This book is a direct result of my upbringing by two amazing parents, Richard and Carol Bracken O'Leary who are looking down on me from heaven. They raised us with a healthy dose of skepticism and respect for ethics.

I would like to acknowledge my dear departed cousin Jody Murphy, an inspirational figure in my life. I am indebted to my beautiful cousin, Nancy Clare Murphy, for unknowingly starting me on this unexpected adventure.

I want to give my heartfelt thanks to my reading team who acted as a focus group for my writing as I moved through the process:

Ron Books, a brilliant CEO of a software company in Texas who gave generously of his time and keen intellect to keep the ideas and mystery flowing and most importantly, keeping me on topic. You are a true friend in every sense of the word. Thanks, brother.

Dr. Mark Maffet, one of the top orthopedic and sports injury surgeons in USA. Mark's prolific mental capacity helped shape the flow of certain chapters and impacted the "page turner" quality of the final book. Dr. Maffet's generosity is exceeded only by his exquisite taste in women.

David Landsidle, a retired lobbyist, a good friend and in-law. Thanks for keeping the book honest and balanced.

Zane Fisher, my lifelong friend and college roommate from Indiana University of Pennsylvania. I really appreciate the long reading sessions and catching things that I had missed.

SPYGATE

I know you have a busy life and I appreciate you taking the time to help.

A cluster of other readers in no particular order: Dennis Noon, Beth O'Leary, Cole Bodell, Christopher Noon, Richard Arredondo, Michael Counter, Tim Gleason and Glenn O'Connor. Thanks, y'all! Your input made the book a more clear and enjoyable read.

Dr. Miao Zang, an extremely intelligent and thoughtful man. A new father, who gave generously of his time and expertise. His wife, also a PhD in Statistical Science, gave birth while we were writing this book. I think that is good luck, is it not Big Cat? The Doctor's first name is pronounced "me-ow" so I called him Big Cat! It makes him laugh.

A special thank you to Professor Lynne Stokes at Southern Methodist University, Statistical Science department and her classes, that participated in looking over some of my studies. I really appreciate you taking the time to discuss the book and its conclusions.

Wayne Allyn Root, the King of Las Vegas Gaming. It is not often that the best at anything in the world will give so generously of his time, to a new writer, especially when that man runs five companies. Your consideration and candor were worth everything to this book. I can't thank you enough; you're a prince and a gentleman.

Matthew Shadonix, my attorney and most trusted consigliore. Your advice and keen wit was most valued; you are like family to me.

My sister-in-law, Andra Cobb, a very talented and beautiful woman, who created all of the art inside and the "camera man" logo for this book cover. Thank you for your long hours!

Book designer, Anthony Sclavi, a true artist. Your help was always professional and consultative. The look of this book is all Anthony. Martha Cobb, an incredibly good proofreader who misses nothing. And finally, my heartfelt appreciation to my editor Anna Nething. As you have just read, a lady of considerable talent.

Family–

A big kiss to Gerry O'Connor for these encouraging words,

"Don't let anyone tell you, you can't write that book!"

To the boys and gals on the Island (near Oakmont, PA), for always being in my corner. You can leave the Island, but it never leaves you. I want to recognize the men in the 12 Mile Island Fantasy Football League, the greatest concentration of football idiots in the known universe.

Thanks to the Bracken Clan spread far and wide. The Irish eyes are smiling and singing! Much gratitude, for all your love and guidance.

Appendix A
All Endnotes

Section I

Chapter 1

[1] Mortensen, Chris. "Sources: Goodell Determines Pats Broke Rules by Taping Jets' Signals." ESPN, September 13, 2007. http://sports.espn.go.com/nfl/news/story?id=3014677

[2] Sando, Mike. "What's Legal, What's Illegal in NFL Spy Game." ESPN, September 13, 2007. http://sports.espn.go.com/nfl/columns/story?columnist=sando_mike&id=3017542

[3] ESPN.com News Services. "Belichick Draws $500,000 Fine, But Avoids Suspension." ESPN, September 14, 2007. http://sports.espn.go.com/nfl/news/story?id=3018338

[4] ESPN.com News Services. "Belichick Issues Apology, Says He's Spoken with Goodell." ESPN, September 13, 2007. http://sports.espn.go.com/nfl/news/story?id=3015478

[5] National Football League. "NFL Rulebook." 2012. http://www.nfl.com/rulebook

[6] Branch, John and Greg Bishop. "New Claim of Taping Emerges Against Patriots." *The New York Times*, February 22, 2008. http://www.nytimes.com/2008/02/22/sports/football/22patriots.html?_r=2

[7] Gasper, Christopher L. "Specter Calls for Independent Investigation." *Boston Globe*, May 14, 2008. http://www.boston.com/sports/football/patriots/reiss_pieces/2008/05/specter_calls_f.html

[8] Belichick, Bill. "Eye to Eye: Bill Belichick," interview by Armen Keteyian, CBS News, September 20, 2007. http://www.youtube.com/watch?v=Hyg9BhqESxU

[9] Clayton, John. "Tape Runs Out on Patriots; Dungy Calls Incident 'Sad.'" ESPN.com, September 14, 2007. http://sports.espn.go.com/nfl/news/story?id=3019280

[10] U.S. Congress. Senate. Senator Arlen Specter of Pennsylvania speaking on New England Patriots Videotaping. 110th Cong., 2nd sess. *Congressional Record* (May 14, 2008), vol. 154, pt. 79:S4175–S4177.

[11] Fish, Mike. "Former Patriots Video Assistant Hints at Team's Spying History." ESPN, February 1, 2008. http://sports.espn.go.com/nfl/news/story?id=3226465

[12] Smith, Michael. "Sources: Patriots Give Belichick Long-Term Extension." ESPN, September 17, 2007. http://sports.espn.go.com/nfl/news/story?id=3023193

Chapter 2

[1] Fish, Mike. "Specter: Goodell's Spygate Explanations Don't Pass Scrutiny." ESPN, February 15, 2008. http://sports.espn.go.com/nfl/news/story?id=3246788

[2] Fish, Mike. "Senator Wants to Know Why NFL Destroyed Patriots Spy Tapes." ESPN, February 2, 2008. http://sports.espn.go.com/nfl/news/story?id=3225539

[3] ESPN.com News Services. "Specter Criticizes NFL, Wants Independent Spygate Investigation." ESPN, May 15, 2008. http://sports.espn.go.com/nfl/news/story?id=3395829

[4] ESPN.com News Services. "Goodell Proposes Plan Making Cheating Penalties Easier to Impose." ESPN, March 7, 2008. http://sports.espn.go.com/nfl/news/story?id=3280996

[5] ESPN.com. "Timeline of Events and Disclosures During Spygate Saga." ESPN, May 12, 2008. http://sports.espn.go.com/nfl/news/story?id=3392047

[6] Easterbrook, Gregg. "Belichick's Cheating Could Lead to Dark Days for NFL." ESPN, October 10, 2007. http://sports.espn.go.com/espn/page2/story?page=easterbrook/070918

[7] Zimmerman, Paul. "Smooth Criminals: Patriots Bring Cheating in the NFL into Modern Era." *Sports Illustrated*, September 13, 2007. http://sportsillustrated.cnn.com/2007/writers/dr_z/09/13/cheating/index.html

[8] Bishop, Greg. "Specter Raises New Questions on Spying." *The New York Times*, March 9, 2008. http://www.nytimes.com/2008/03/09/sports/football/09nfl.html

[9] Fish, Mike. "Walsh's Attorney Says NFL Indemnification Offer Falls Short." ESPN, February 15, 2008. http://sports.espn.go.com/nfl/news/story?id=3248267

[10] Clayton, John "Kraft, Belichick Address Owners, Apologize for Spygate." ESPN, April 1, 2008. http://sports.espn.go.com/nfl/news/story?id=3323437

[11] "NFL Owners Meetings: Kraft Apologizes For Spygate Scandal." *Sports Business Journal Daily*, April 2, 2008. http://www.sportsbusinessdaily.com/Daily/Issues/2008/04/Issue-133/Leagues-Governing-Bodies/NFL-Owners-Meetings-Kraft-Apologizes-For-Spygate-Scandal.aspx

[12] Branch, John and Greg Bishop. "New Claim of Taping Emerges Against Patriots." *The New York Times*, February 22, 2008. http://www.nytimes.com/2008/02/22/sports/football/22patriots.html?_r=2

[13] Clayton, John. "Goodell Could Get Another Tool to Defend Sport." ESPN, March 18, 2008. http://sports.espn.go.com/nfl/columns/story?columnist=clayton_john&id=3320938

[14] Harris, John. "Rooney: Spygate 'Had No Impact' in Losses to Patriots." *Tribune-Review*, February 15, 2008. http://www.pittsburghlive.com/x/pittsburghtrib/s_552617.html

[15] Daily News Staff Writer. "Robert Kraft Apologizes for SpyGate; Bill Belichick Misinterpreted Rule." *New York Daily News*, April 2, 2008. http://articles.nydailynews.com/2008-04-02/sports/17895302_1_defensive-signals-bill-belichick-questions-so-many-times

[16] Monkovic, Toni. "Rodger Goodell Interview Transcript." *The New York Times*, May 1, 2008. http://fifthdown.blogs.nytimes.com/2008/05/01/roger-goodell-transcript/

Section II

Chapter 3

[1] Junipero Serra High School. "2004 Athletic Hall of Fame Inductees." 2010. http://www.serrahs.com/page.cfm?p=2552

² Montville, Leigh. "Golden Boy." *Sports Illustrated*, August 3, 1998. http://sportsillustrated.cnn.com/vault/article/magazine/MAG1013468/index.htm

³ Halberstam, David. *The Education of a Coach*. New York: Hyperion, 2005.

⁴ National Football League. "NFL Rulebook." 2012. http://www.nfl.com/rulebook

⁵ Pro-Football-Reference.com. "Pro Football Statistics and History." 2012. http://www.pro-football-reference.com/

⁶ Belichick, Bill. Interview by Mike Greenberg and Mike Golic, in "Mike and Mike in the Morning." ESPN Boston Radio, December 2, 2011.

Chapter 4

¹ Halberstam, David. *The Education of a Coach*. New York: Hyperion, 2005, 115-16.

² McEntegart, Pete. "The 10 Spot." *Sports Illustrated*, July 28, 2006. http://sportsillustrated.cnn.com/vault/article/web/COM1055750/index.htm

³ Associated Press. "Belichick Quits as Jets Coach." CBS News, February 11, 2009. http://www.cbsnews.com/2100-500609_162-146017.html

Chapter 5

[1] Hohler, Bob. "Adams's Role? It's Top Secret." *Boston Globe*, February 3, 2008. http://boston.com/sports/football/patriots/articles/2008/02/03/adamss_role_its_top_secret/

[2] Halberstam, David. *The Education of a Coach*. New York: Hyperion, 2005.

[3] Thompson, Wright. "Who Is This Guy?" ESPN, 2009. http://sports.espn.go.com/espn/eticket/story?page=adams

[4] Warren, Tim. "Mystery Man." *Northwestern Magazine*, Winter 2008. http://www.northwestern.edu/magazine/winter2008/feature/adams.html

[5] Sando, Mike. "What's Legal, What's Illegal in NFL Spy Game." ESPN, September 13, 2007. http://sports.espn.go.com/nfl/columns/story?columnist=sando_mike&id=3017542

[6] Bouchette, Ed. "The Elephant in the Stadium: Spygate's Cloud of Innuendo Still Dogs Patriots." *Pittsburgh Post-Gazette*, February 5, 2012. http://old.post-gazette.com/pg/12036/1208250-66-0.stm

SPYGATE

Section III

Chapter 6

[1] Fish, Mike. "Former Patriots Video Assistant Hints at Team's Spying History." ESPN, February 1, 2008. http://sports.espn.go.com/nfl/news/story?id=3226465

[2] Walsh, Matt. Interview by Andrea Kremer, in "HBO Real Sports with Bryant Gumbel." HBO, May 16, 2008.

[3] ESPN.com News Services. "Walsh Dismisses Pats' Attempts to Minimize Illegal Taping." ESPN, May 15, 2008. http://sports.espn.go.com/nfl/news/story?id=3396731

[4] Zimmerman, Paul. "Smooth Criminals: Patriots Bring Cheating in the NFL into Modern Era." *Sports Illustrated*, September 13, 2007. http://sportsillustrated.cnn.com/2007/writers/dr_z/09/13/cheating/index.html

[5] Fish, Mike. "One Tape Turned Over by Walsh Shows Patriots Also Stole Offensive Signals." ESPN, May 9, 2008. http://sports.espn.go.com/nfl/columns/story?columnist=fish_mike&id=3387401

[6] Associated Press. "Matt Walsh to Meet with Goodell, Specter on Tuesday." USA Today, May 13, 2008. http://www.usatoday.com/sports/football/nfl/2008-05-12-walsh-meetings_N.htm

[7] Fish, Mike. "NFL, Ex-Pats Video Assistant Walsh Finally Agree to Spygate Meeting." ESPN, April 24, 2008. http://sports.espn.go.com/nfl/news/story?id=3363455

[8] Associated Press. "Walsh Meets with Goodell, Specter." YES Network, May 13, 2008. http://web.yesnetwork.com/news/article.jsp?ymd=20080513&content_id=1443062&vkey=1

[9] Gasper, Christopher L. "Specter Calls for Independent Investigation." *Boston Globe*, May 14, 2008. http://www.boston.com/sports/football/patriots/reiss_pieces/2008/05/specter_calls_f.html

[10] U.S. Congress. Senate. Senator Arlen Specter of Pennsylvania speaking on New England Patriots Videotaping. 110th Cong., 2nd sess. *Congressional Record* (May 14, 2008), vol. 154, pt. 79:S4175–S4177.

Chapter 7

[1] Thompson, Wright. "Who Is This Guy?" ESPN, 2009. http://sports.espn.go.com/espn/eticket/story?page=adams

[2] Belichick, Bill. "Eye to Eye: Bill Belichick," interview by Armen Keteyian, CBS News, September 20, 2007. http://www.youtube.com/watch?v=Hyg9BhqESxU

3 Mortensen, Chris. "Sources: Goodell Determines Pats Broke Rules by Taping Jets' Signals." ESPN, September 13, 2007. http://sports.espn.go.com/nfl/news/story?id=3014677

4 Walsh, Matt. Interview by Andrea Kremer, in "HBO Real Sports with Bryant Gumbel." HBO, May 16, 2008.

5 Halberstam, David. *The Education of a Coach*. New York: Hyperion, 2005.

6 Das, Andrew. "I Spy a Problem." *The New York Times*, March 7, 2008. http://fifthdown.blogs.nytimes.com/2008/03/07/i-spy-a-problem/

7 Le Batard, Dan. "The Dan Le Batard Show." 790 AM *The Ticket*, February 1, 2008.

8 ESPN.com. "Timeline of Events and Disclosures During Spygate Saga." ESPN, May 12, 2008. http://sports.espn.go.com/nfl/news/story?id=3392047

9 Christenbury, Jeff. "Ted Johnson: I Received Opposing Teams' Audibles." *Sports of Boston*, February 22, 2008. http://sportsofboston.com/2008/02/22/ted-johnson-i-received-opposing-teams-audibles/

[10] King, Peter. "Giants' Tuck: Stopping Vick 'Almost Impossible', Plus 10 Things to Watch." *Sports Illustrated*, November 19, 2010. http://sportsillustrated.cnn.com/2010/writers/peter_king/11/19/giants-eagles/index.html

[11] Smith, Michael David. "Eric Mangini has 'a lot of regrets' about Spygate." NBC Sports, September 13, 2011. http://profootballtalk.nbcsports.com/2011/09/13/eric-mangini-has-a-lot-of-regrets-about-spygate/

[12] Young, Steve. Interview by Dan Patrick, in "The Dan Patrick Radio Show." May 16, 2008. http://http-trd-l3.cdn.turner.com/si/danpatrick/audio/2008/05/16/DP-Steve_Young%20-5-16_Interview.mp3?eref=fromSI

Chapter 8

[1] Battista, Judy. "Coach Follows Dream to Football's Summit." *The New York Times*, January 30, 2008. http://www.nytimes.com/2008/01/30/sports/football/30patriots.html

[2] Brady, Tom. Interview on WEEI Radio. November 21, 2007.

SPYGATE

[3] Fallon, Julie. "Broncos Spygate 2: Will the bingers be pointed at Bill Belichick again?" *The Christian Science Monitor*, November 29, 2010. http://www.csmonitor.com/USA/Sports/2010/1129/Broncos-Spygate-2-Will-the-fingers-be-pointed-at-Bill-Belichick-again

[4] Couch, Greg. "Broncos' Spygate Reeks of Cover-Up." AOL News, November 27, 2010. http://www.aolnews.com/2010/11/27/broncos-spygate-reeks-of-cover-up/

[5] Florio, Mike. "Report: McDaniels Explains to Coaching Staff Differences Between Spygate I and II." NBC Sports, November 28, 2010. http://profootballtalk.nbcsports.com/2010/11/28/report-mcdaniels-explains-to-coaching-staff-differences-between-spygate-i-and-ii/

[6] Klis, Mike. "McDaniels Fired as Broncos Coach After Controversy, Losses Pile Up." *The Denver Post*, December 6, 2010. http://www.denverpost.com/broncos/ci_16791509

Chapter 9

[1] McLuskey, Dex and Aaron Kuriloff. "NFL Signs Nine-Year Extensions of Television Contracts With CBS, FOX, NBC." *Bloomberg*, December 14, 2011. http://www.bloomberg.com/news/2011-12-14/nfl-renews-television-contracts-with-cbs-fox-nbc-networks-through-2022.html

[2] Badenhausen, Kurt, Michael K. Ozanian and Christina Settimi, eds. "Football's Most Valuable Teams." *Forbes*, September 7, 2011. http://www.forbes.com/lists/2011/30/nfl-valuations-11_land.html

[3] Pasquarelli, Len. "Brady Now Among the NFL's Highest-Paid Players." ESPN, May 8, 2005. http://sports.espn.go.com/nfl/columns/story?columnist=pasquarelli_len&id=2054072

[4] King, Peter. "Another Patriots Victory." *Sports Illustrated*, May 9, 2005. http://sportsillustrated.cnn.com/2005/writers/peter_king/05/08/mmqb.brady/

[5] Smith, Michael. "Sources: Patriots Give Belichick Long-Term Extension." ESPN, September 17, 2007. http://sports.espn.go.com/nfl/news/story?id=3023193

Section IV

Background for Statisical Analysis

[1] Belichick, Bill. "Eye to Eye: Bill Belichick," interview by Armen Keteyian, CBS News, September 20, 2007. http://www.youtube.com/watch?v=Hyg9BhqESxU

SPYGATE

Conclusion

[1] King, Peter. "The Man of the Hour." *Sports Illustrated*, February 7, 2011. http://sportsillustrated.cnn.com/vault/article/magazine/MAG1181467/index.htm

[2] Reiss, Mike. "Patriots Never Taped Walkthrough, Goodell Finds." *Boston Globe*, May 14, 2008. http://articles.boston.com/2008-05-14/sports/29274687_1_roger-goodell-tape-videotaping

[3] Brinson, Will. "Report: Goodell's Salary to 'Double' Up to $20M." CBS Sports, February 13, 2012. http://www.cbssports.com/mcc/blogs/entry/22475988/34822324

[4] Myers, Gary. "Don Shula: Spygate Would Mar Pats' Undefeated Season." *New York Daily News*, November 6, 2007. http://www.nydailynews.com/sports/football/don-shula-spygate-mar-pats-undefeated-season-article-1.255721

Appendix B
Catalog of Figures and Tables

Figures

Figure 1: Scatter Plot of Average Home Wins 2001-2011, page 206

Figure 2: Histogram of Average Home Wins 2001-2011, page 208

Figure 3: Histogram of Average ATS 2001-2011, page 227

Figure 4: Scatter Plot of Average ATS 2001-2011, page 228

Tables

Table 1: Chances of All Possible Outcomes of Binomial Question, page 215

Appendix C
NFL Home Records 2001–2011

		2001	2002	2003	2004	2005	2006	2007	2008	2009	2010	2011	Average
New England	W	6	5	8	8	5	5	8	5	8	8	7	6.64
	L	2	3	0	0	3	3	0	3	0	0	1	
NY Jets	W	3	5	4	6	4	4	3	5	4	5	6	4.45
	L	5	3	4	2	4	4	5	3	4	3	2	
Miami	W	7	7	4	3	5	4	1	5	4	1	4	4.09
	L	1	1	4	5	3	4	7	3	4	7	4	
Buffalo	W	1	5	4	5	4	4	4	3	3	2	5	3.64
	L	7	3	4	3	4	4	4	5	5	6	3	
Indianapolis	W	3	5	5	7	7	8	6	7	7	6	2	5.73
	L	5	3	3	1	1	0	2	1	1	2	6	
Houston	W	na	2	3	3	2	4	6	6	4	5	5	4.00
	L		6	5	5	6	4	2	2	4	3	3	
Jacksonville	W	3	3	5	4	6	6	6	2	5	4	4	4.36
	L	5	5	3	4	2	2	2	6	3	4	4	
Pittsburgh	W	7	5	4	8	5	5	7	6	6	5	7	5.91
	L	1	2	4	0	3	3	1	2	2	3	1	
Cleveland	W	4	3	2	3	4	2	7	1	3	3	3	3.18
	L	4	5	6	5	4	6	1	7	5	5	5	
Cincinnati	W	4	1	5	5	5	4	5	3	6	3	4	4.09
	L	4	7	3	3	3	4	3	4	2	5	4	
Baltimore	W	6	4	7	5	6	7	4	6	6	7	8	6.00
	L	2	4	1	3	2	1	4	2	2	1	0	

		2001	2002	2003	2004	2005	2006	2007	2008	2009	2010	2011	Average
Oakland	W	5	6	4	3	2	2	2	2	2	5	3	3.27
	L	3	2	4	5	6	6	6	6	6	3	5	
San Diego	W	4	5	2	7	4	6	7	5	6	6	5	5.36
	L	4	3	6	1	4	8	1	3	2	2	3	
Kansas City	W	3	6	8	4	7	6	2	1	1	7	3	4.36
	L	5	2	0	4	1	2	6	7	7	1	5	
Denver	W	6	5	6	6	8	4	5	4	4	3	3	4.91
	L	2	3	2	2	0	4	3	4	4	5	5	
Seattle	W	5	3	8	5	8	5	7	2	4	5	4	5.09
	L	3	5	0	3	0	3	1	6	4	3	4	
Arizona	W	3	3	4	5	3	3	6	6	4	4	6	4.27
	L	5	5	4	3	5	5	2	2	4	4	2	
Philadelphia	W	4	7	5	7	4	5	3	6	6	4	3	4.91
	L	4	1	3	1	4	3	5	2	2	4	5	
NY Giants	W	6	5	1	3	7	3	3	7	4	5	4	4.36
	L	2	3	7	5	1	5	5	1	4	3	4	
Washington	W	4	5	3	3	6	3	5	4	3	2	2	3.64
	L	4	3	5	5	2	5	3	4	5	6	6	
Dallas	W	4	4	6	4	5	4	6	6	6	2	5	4.73
	L	4	4	2	4	3	4	2	2	2	6	3	
Minnesota	W	5	4	6	5	6	3	5	6	8	4	1	4.82
	L	3	4	2	3	2	5	3	2	0	4	7	

		2001	2002	2003	2004	2005	2006	2007	2008	2009	2010	2011	Average
Chicago	W	7	3	6	2	7	6	4	6	5	5	5	5.09
	L	1	5	2	6	1	2	4	2	3	3	3	
Detroit	W	2	3	5	3	3	2	5	0	2	4	5	3.09
	L	5	5	3	5	5	6	3	8	6	4	3	
Green Bay	W	7	**8**	5	4	3	3	7	4	6	7	**8**	5.64
	L	1	**0**	3	4	5	5	1	4	2	1	**0**	
Tampa Bay	W	5	6	3	4	6	3	6	6	1	4	3	4.27
	L	3	2	5	4	2	5	2	2	7	4	5	
Atlanta	W	3	5	2	7	4	3	3	7	6	7	6	4.82
	L	5	3	6	1	4	5	5	1	2	1	2	
New Orleans	W	3	4	5	3	1	4	3	6	6	5	**8**	4.36
	L	5	4	3	5	7	4	5	2	2	3	**0**	
Carolina	W	0	4	6	3	5	4	2	**8**	5	2	3	3.82
	L	8	4	2	5	3	4	6	**0**	3	6	5	
San Fran	W	5	5	6	1	3	4	3	4	6	5	7	4.45
	L	3	3	2	7	5	4	5	4	2	3	1	
St. Louis	W	6	6	**8**	6	3	4	1	1	0	5	1	3.73
	L	2	2	**0**	2	5	4	7	7	8	3	7	
Tennessee	W	3	6	7	2	3	4	5	7	5	3	5	4.55
	L	5	2	1	6	5	4	3	1	3	5	3	

10 year NFL Average HW: 4.55
10 Year Standard Deviation: 0.84

Appendix D
ATS NFL Wins 2001–2011

ATS		2001	2002	2003	2004	2005	2006	2007	2008	2009	2010	2011	Totals	Net Wins ATS
Arizona	Win	9	6	6	9	6	8	9	9	8	5	8	83	-6
	Loss	6	10	10	7	9	8	7	7	7	11	7	89	
	Tie	1				1				1		1	4	
Atlanta	Win	6	10	6	7	8	8	8	9	11	11	7	91	11
	Loss	8	6	10	8	8	8	8	7	5	5	7	80	
	Tie	2			1							2	5	
Baltimore	Win	8	10	9	9	7	10	3	12	8	8	8	92	13
	Loss	7	6	6	7	9	6	13	4	7	7	7	79	
	Tie	1		1						1	1	1	5	
Buffalo	Win	6	8	6	10	7	10	10	7	8	8	6	86	3
	Loss	10	6	9	5	9	6	6	9	7	7	9	83	
	Tie		2	1	1					1	1	1	7	
Carolina	Win	7	10	6	9	9	5	8	9	9	4	9	85	-1
	Loss	8	6	10	6	7	9	8	6	7	12	7	86	
	Tie	1			1		2		1				5	
Chicago	Win	11	5	8	6	9	10	7	6	6	9	7	84	-1
	Loss	5	11	8	9	5	6	9	8	10	6	8	85	
	Tie				1	2			2		1	1	7	
Cincinnati	Win	8	4	9	7	8	8	6	7	7	7	8	79	-13
	Loss	8	12	6	9	8	7	9	9	9	9	6	92	
	Tie			1		0	1	1				2	5	
Cleveland	Win	7	11	6	6	8	8	12	7	10	5	8	88	7
	Loss	7	4	10	10	8	7	4	9	6	10	6	81	
	Tie	2	1				1				1	2	7	
Dallas	Win	8	8	9	7	7	8	9	7	9	6	5	83	-4
	Loss	8	7	6	9	7	7	7	9	7	10	10	87	
	Tie		1	1		2	1					1	6	
Denver	Win	7	7	8	6	11	5	5	4	9	6	7	75	-19
	Loss	9	8	8	7	4	11	11	11	7	10	8	94	
	Tie		1	1	3	1			1			1	8	
Detroit	Win	8	7	9	8	9	6	6	7	4	12	7	83	-4
	Loss	7	9	7	7	7	10	9	9	10	4	8	87	
	Tie	1			1			1		2		1	6	

ATS		2001	2002	2003	2004	2005	2006	2007	2008	2009	2010	2011	Totals	Net Wins ATS
Green Bay	Win	9	8	10	7	5	7	12	8	11	9	11	97	25
	Loss	7	8	6	8	9	7	3	8	4	7	5	72	
	Tie				1	2	2	1		1			7	
Houston	Win		7	9	8	7	7	8	8	7	5	10	76	-2
	Loss		8	7	7	9	9	8	7	8	10	5	78	
	Tie		1		1	0			1	1	1	1	6	
Indianapolis	Win	6	6	10	9	9	7	9	7	10	8	6	87	4
	Loss	10	10	5	6	6	8	7	8	6	7	10	83	
	Tie			1	1	1	1		1		1		6	
Jacksonville	Win	7	8	7	10	9	8	11	4	5	9	7	85	-1
	Loss	8	8	9	6	5	7	5	12	11	7	8	86	
	Tie	1				2	1					1	5	
Kansas City	Win	7	8	10	6	9	8	7	8	7	9	9	88	7
	Loss	7	6	6	10	5	8	8	8	9	7	7	81	
	Tie	2	2			2		1					7	
Miami	Win	10	9	7	7	7	6	5	8	8	8	9	84	-4
	Loss	5	7	9	9	9	10	9	8	8	8	6	88	
	Tie	1						2				1	4	
Minnesota	Win	6	8	8	7	9	7	7	10	9	6	6	83	-5
	Loss	10	8	8	9	7	9	7	6	6	10	8	88	
	Tie							2		1		2	5	
New England	Win	11	6	13	11	8	9	10	9	8	10	9	104	38
	Loss	5	10	2	3	8	7	6	7	7	5	6	66	
	Tie			1	2		0			1	1	1	6	
New Orleans	Win	6	8	9	8	5	10	6	10	8	6	12	88	3
	Loss	10	7	7	8	10	6	10	5	8	10	4	85	
	Tie		1			1			1				3	
NY Giants	Win	6	9	3	8	10	7	10	12	6	7	8	86	2
	Loss	9	7	11	8	5	8	6	4	10	9	7	84	
	Tie	1		2		1	1					1	6	
NY Jets	Win	8	9	5	8	6	11	6	7	9	9	6	84	-2
	Loss	8	6	8	7	10	5	9	9	7	7	10	86	
	Tie		1	3	1			1					6	

ATS		2001	2002	2003	2004	2005	2006	2007	2008	2009	2010	2011	Totals	Net Wins ATS
Oakland	Win	7	10	3	6	5	6	6	7	8	8	9	75	-20
	Loss	7	6	12	9	10	10	10	9	8	8	6	95	
	Tie	1		1	1	1						1	5	
Philadelphia	Win	11	10	11	9	5	8	8	10	9	8	8	97	21
	Loss	4	6	4	7	11	7	8	6	7	8	8	76	
	Tie	1		1			1						3	
Pittsburgh	Win	11	5	8	11	9	7	8	9	5	10	7	90	7
	Loss	4	10	8	5	7	9	8	7	10	6	9	83	
	Tie	1	1				0			1			3	
San Diego	Win	4	9	6	13	9	9	11	7	8	8	6	90	12
	Loss	10	7	10	1	6	7	5	8	7	7	10	78	
	Tie	2			2	1			1	1	1		8	
San Francisco	Win	9	4	7	6	8	9	5	7	9	7	11	82	-2
	Loss	6	10	7	10	8	7	11	8	4	9	4	84	
	Tie	1	2	2					1	3		1	10	
Seattle	Win	5	9	8	5	9	6	6	7	6	7	10	78	-11
	Loss	8	7	7	11	6	9	9	8	10	9	5	89	
	Tie	3		1		1	1	1	1			1	9	
St. Louis	Win	9	4	9	6	5	8	5	6	7	10	3	72	-28
	Loss	6	12	6	10	11	7	11	10	9	6	12	100	
	Tie	1		1			1					1	4	
Tampa	Win	6	10	6	5	8	6	8	8	6	9	4	76	-17
	Loss	9	6	9	10	8	9	7	8	10	5	12	93	
	Tie	1		1	1		1	1			2	0	7	
Tennessee	Win	6	10	9	5	6	11	8	12	6	8	6	87	1
	Loss	10	6	7	11	10	5	7	4	9	8	9	86	
	Tie							1		1		1	3	
Washington	Win	8	7	7	8	9	5	7	6	7	8	7	79	-3
	Loss	7	8	7	8	6	9	8	8	8	5	9	82	
	Tie	1	1	2		1	2	2	2	1	3		15